U0483735

符号中国 SIGNS OF CHINA

茶马古道

ANCIENT TEA-HORSE ROAD

"符号中国"编写组 ◎ 编著

中央民族大学出版社
China Minzu University Press

图书在版编目(CIP)数据

茶马古道：汉文、英文 /"符号中国"编写组编著. —北京：
中央民族大学出版社，2024.9
（符号中国）
ISBN 978-7-5660-2317-9

Ⅰ.①茶…　Ⅱ.①符…　Ⅲ.①古道－介绍－中国－汉、英　Ⅳ.①K928.78

中国国家版本馆CIP数据核字（2024）第016651号

符号中国：**茶马古道** ANCIENT TEA-HORSE ROAD

编　　著	"符号中国"编写组
策划编辑	沙　平
责任编辑	黄修义
英文编辑	邱　械
美术编辑	曹　娜　郑亚超　洪　涛
出版发行	中央民族大学出版社
	北京市海淀区中关村南大街27号　　邮编：100081
	电话：（010）68472815（发行部）　传真：（010）68933757（发行部）
	（010）68932218（总编室）　　　　（010）68932447（办公室）
经销者	全国各地新华书店
印刷厂	北京兴星伟业印刷有限公司
开　　本	787 mm×1092 mm　1/16　印张：10.75
字　　数	149千字
版　　次	2024年9月第1版　2024年9月第1次印刷
书　　号	ISBN 978-7-5660-2317-9
定　　价	58.00元

版权所有　侵权必究

"符号中国"丛书编委会

唐兰东　巴哈提　杨国华　孟靖朝　赵秀琴

本册编写者

刘　勇

前言 Preface

在中国西南部的山川中，绵延盘旋着一条神秘的古道——马蹄印深嵌在高山悬崖边的石板上，高悬的铁索吊桥下是湍急的河流……这是一条由驮运货物的马帮踏出的通道，这就是茶马古道。

茶马古道"因茶而盛，为马而生"，源自中国西南地区1300多年前

Winding through mountains in southwest China, there is a mysterious ancient road — with deep hoof prints imbedded on the narrow trails of high cliff edges and turbulent rivers flowing under high suspending chain bridges … This is a passage treaded by caravans, the Ancient Tea-horse Road.

Originated in the ancient "Tea-horse Mutual Trade" in southwest China, the Ancient Tea-horse Road " ourished because of tea, and

的"茶马互市",马匹是古道上主要交通工具。茶马古道和中国古代丝绸之路一样,不但是一条贸易通道,也是民族文化交流的大走廊,有着深厚的文化内涵。

茶马古道应该说是世界上地势最高,路况最险,距离最长的千年古道,充满着神秘与传奇色彩。本书以图文并茂的形式,探寻茶马古道的形成过程,生动地展现了古道沿途的壮丽风光,以及各民族的民俗风情等,希望读者由此更好地了解茶马古道。

was born because of horses". Even in modern times, horse caravans are still an important transportation means on this ancient road. Same as the Silk Road in ancient times, the Tea-horse Road served not only as a route for trade, but also a thoroughfare for ethnic cultural exchanges. So the Road bears profound cultural significance.

It is no exaggeration to say that this one-thousand-year-old Tea-horse Road is of the highest elevation, the most precipitous conditions and the longest distance in the world. The Road is full of mysteries and legends. Through texts and pictures, the book explores the history of this ancient road, presents the magnificent landscape and beautiful scenery, and introduces ethnic customs of people living along the Road. It is our sincerest hope that all these elements contribute to a better understanding of the Ancient Tea-horse Road.

目录 Contents

古道沧桑
Vicissitudes of the Ancient Tea-horse Road...................... 001

唐宋的茶马互市
Tea-horse Mutual Trade during the Tang and
Song Dynasties.. 002

元明清的繁荣
Prosperity during the Yuan, Ming and Qing Dynasties 008

近现代的盛衰
Rise and Fall in Modern and Contemporary Times........... 013

古道寻踪
Traces of the Ancient Tea-horse Road........................... 017

茶马古道之滇藏道
Yunnan-Xizang Route of the Ancient Tea-horse Road....... 018

茶马古道之川藏道
Sichuan-Xizang Route of the Ancient Tea-horse Road 022

马帮与脚夫
Caravans and Porters.. 026

古道茶香
Tea Aroma on the Ancient Tea-horse Road 039

茶马古道上的茶
Tea on the Ancient Tea-horse Road 040

古道民族与茶俗
People Living along the Ancient Tea-horse Road and Their
Tea Drinking Habits.. 055

古道驿镇
Towns on the Ancient Tea-horse Road............................. 093

茶叶发源之地西双版纳
Xishuangbanna: Place of Origin of Tea 094

普洱茶的源头和集散地普洱
Pu'er: Place of Origin and Distribution Center of Pu'er Tea 101

古城大理
Dali: A Beautiful Ancient Town 104

土司故地丽江
Lijiang: Former Residence of Aboriginal Office 109

人间仙境香格里拉
Shangri-La: Paradise on Earth 113

雪山集市德钦
Deqin: A Market in Snow Mountains 118

边茶产地雅安
Ya'an: Place of Origin of Border Tea............................... 122

锅庄之城康定
Kangding: Town of Wok Stands (*Guozhuang*) 126

"最后的净土"稻城
Daocheng: "The Last Pure Land on Earth"........................ 131

交通咽喉泸定
Luding: A Transportation I lub... 134

川西门户松潘
Songpan: Gateway to Western Sichuan Province 136

"最高城镇"理塘
Litang: "The Highest City"... 138

古道盐都盐井
Yanjing: Salt Town on the Ancient Road 142

两河交汇之处昌都
Qamdo: Town at the Confluence of Two Rivers 146

日光之城拉萨
Lhasa: The Sunshine City 150

山顶庄园日喀则
Shigatse: A Fertile Farm... 155

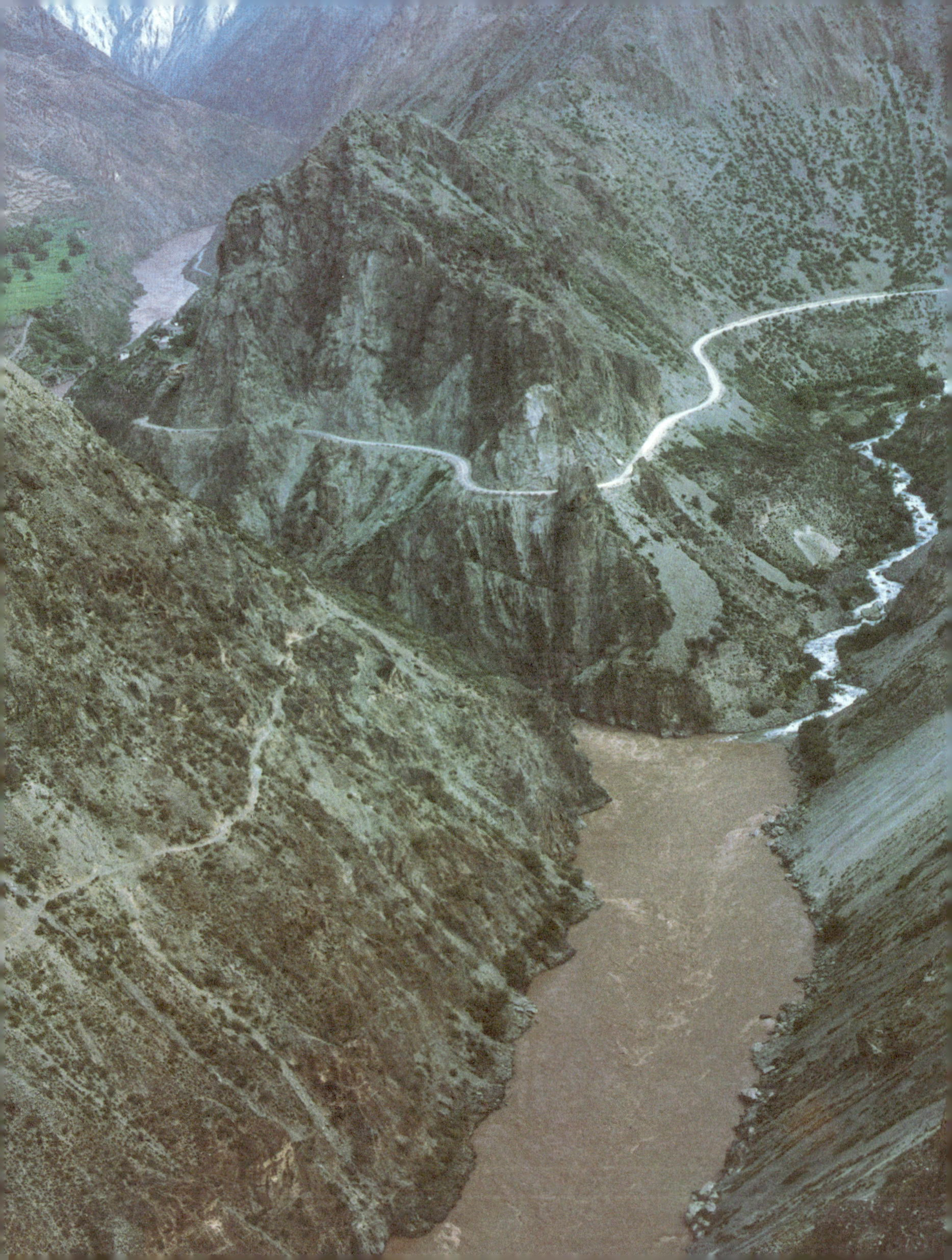

古道沧桑
Vicissitudes of the Ancient Tea-horse Road

　　茶马古道蜿蜒在中国西南部的横断山脉之间，1300多年来，它将云南、四川的茶叶输送到西藏，又将雪域高原的马匹、兽皮、藏药等特产运到内地，促进了内地与西藏的经济文化交流。

Winding through the Hengduan Mountains in southwest China, the Ancient Tea-horse Road has witnessed the trade between Yunnan, Sichuan and Xizang over the past 1,300 years, where tea from Yunnan and Sichuan was shipped to Xizang in exchange of Xizang's horses, furs, herbs and other native produce. Indeed the Road has served as a linkage between the Qinghai-Xizang Plateau and the interior by facilitating the economic and cultural exchanges between the two regions.

> 唐宋的茶马互市

> Tea-horse Mutual Trade during the Tang and Song Dynasties

茶马古道起源于古代的"茶马互市",可以说是先有"互市",后有"古道"。茶马互市是历史上汉藏民族间一种传统的以茶易马或以马换茶为内容的贸易往来,始于唐宋时期。作为中国历史上的鼎盛时期,唐朝国家实力的增强,促进了各民族之间的频繁交往,中原民族与西南少数民族之间互市的内容进一步丰富。

唐高祖武德八年(625年),突厥、吐谷浑等西北少数民族请求互市,唐高祖允准,并且派遣使者出使吐谷浑。内地所产的丝织品和茶叶是唐王朝用于互市的主要物品,而牲畜则是少数民族用于互市的主

The Ancient Tea-horse Road had its origin in the Tea-horse Mutual Trade in ancient times. It can be stated that Mutual Trade gave birth to the Ancient Road. First emerged during the Tang and Song dynasties, the Tea-horse Mutual Trade by then was only in the traditional form of barter between the Han people and the Zang people. During the ourishing period of the Tang Dynasty, prompted by its national strength, the government adopted a policy to encourage the exchange between its ethnic groups. As a result, the scale of mutual trade was expanded and diversified between people in the Central Plains and ethnic groups in the southwestern region.

In the 8th year of the Wude Period during the reign of Emperor Gaozu of

要商品。

唐太宗在位期间，青藏高原上的吐蕃人逐渐崛起。贞观十二年（638年），吐蕃首领松赞干布率吐蕃大军进攻大唐边城松州（今四川松潘），唐太宗派大军讨伐，大败

- **唐太宗像**

唐太宗李世民是唐朝的第二位皇帝。他即位后，积极纳谏，励精图治，使社会出现了国泰民安的局面，开创了著名的"贞观之治"。他是历史上最出名的政治家之一。

A Portrait of Emperor Taizong of the Tang Dynasty

Li Shimin, Emperor Taizong was the second emperor of the Tang Dynasty who ruled from 627 to 649. After ascending the throne, Taizong was open to advice and committed to efficient governance, which brought peace and prosperity to the country and the people. His Governance during the Zhenguan Period was considered an innovative and successful period in Chinese history. Taizong was remembered by later generations as one of the most famous politicians in Chinese history.

the Tang Dynasty (625), in response to the request of the Turks, Tuyuhuns and other ethnic groups inhabited in the northwestern region, the Emperor gave his endorsement for mutual trade and sent envoys to the Tuyuhuns territory. Back then, tea and silk products from the interior were the major goods traded for livestock raised by ethnic groups.

During the Zhenguan Period of the Tang Dynasty when Emperor Taizong ruled China, a tribal group on the Qinghai-Xizang Plateau gradually rose. In the 12th year of the Zhenguan Period (638), a army led by its king Songtsän Gampo (617-650), invaded a border town named Songzhou (present day Songpan City, Sichuan Province). This invasion encountered immediate resistance by the troops sent by Emperor Taizong and ended in a complete failure. Defeated by the Tang-dynasty army and stunned by the prosperity of the Great Tang Empire, Songtsän Gampo resigned himself to being a vassalage of the Great Tang. In his letter of repentance to Emperor Taizong, Songtsän Gampo made a special request for a royal marriage to consolidate the tie between the Great Tang and Tubo. Later in the 15th year of the Zhenguan Period (641), Emperor Taizong consented

吐蕃于松州城下。松赞干布俯首称臣，并对大唐的强盛赞慕不已。他在上书谢罪的同时，还特向唐朝求婚，以示血脉交融的联姻之好。贞观十五年（641年），唐太宗应允吐蕃的请求，把16岁的文成公主嫁给松赞干布。文成公主进藏时，带去了大量的庄稼种子、生产工具、医疗器械，以及包括茶叶在内的生活用品，还有经史、诗文、工艺、医药、历法等书籍。

吐蕃最早的饮茶习惯是由到过

to the marriage proposal and sent Princess Wencheng who was sixteen years old, on a wedding journey to Tubo. Along with the royal convoy, Princess Wencheng brought with her a variety of crop seeds, production tools, medical devices, books about history, poems, technology, medicine, calendar, etc., and daily necessities, including tea.

Tea-drinking as a habit, was first introduced to the Tubos, ancestors of the Zang people by local celebrities or elites who had visited the interior or had been rewarded by the Tang-dynasty government, as well as residents living in areas close

- 阎立本《步辇图》（唐）

《步辇图》取材于唐太宗贞观十五年（641年）吐蕃首领松赞干布与文成公主联姻的事件，描绘了唐太宗李世民接见吐蕃使臣禄东赞的情景。

Emperor Taizong's Sedan (Bunian Tu) by Yan Liben (Tang Dynasty, 618-907)

The theme of the painting was based on the historical event of the marriage between the Tubo King Songtsän Gampo and Princess Wencheng of the Tang Dynasty in the 15th year of the Zhenguan Period of Emperor Taizong (641). This painting depicts the scene when Emperor Taizong receives the Tubo envoy Lu Dongzan.

内地或得到大唐赏赐的上层人物，以及生活在靠近内地的藏族聚居区的民众间兴起的。因藏族聚居区属高寒地区，藏民过着以游牧为主的生活，糌粑、奶类、酥油、牛羊肉是当地的主食。过多的脂肪不易消化，而茶叶既能促进消化，又能防止燥热，对藏民身体健康有益，这使当地人逐渐形成饮茶的习惯，茶叶成为生活的必需品。但由于藏族聚居区不产茶，藏汉交界地区的商人即展开以马换茶的易货贸易。

唐代茶马互市的主要通道为"青藏道"，也称为"唐蕃古道"。这条道路东起关中地区（今陕西省），经过青海，从四川西北角过金沙江，经西藏的昌都、那曲至逻些（今拉萨市）。

而从五代到宋代初年，由于内地战乱频仍，需要从藏族聚居区采购很多战马。同时，为了以茶叶贸易来密切与藏族聚居区各部落的关系，朝廷正式建立起了"以茶易马"的互市制度，使茶叶输藏成为朝廷专管的一项国策。作为茶马互市的必经之路，茶马古道也随之有了较大的拓展。

to the interior. As some areas inhabited by Zang people are in the alpine region, ancient Zang people led a nomadic life. They dined mostly on tsampa, milk, butter, beef and mutton. Such a diet contained much fat which was difficult to digest. Tea could not only help with the digestion system, but also help release excessive body heat. Tea-drinking gradually became a habit as well as a daily necessity of local people. As tea had never been cultivated in the areas inhabited by Zang people, merchants started the barter trade of horses for tea.

Back in the Tang Dynasty, the Qinghai-Xizang Route (also known as the Ancient Tang-Tubo Route) was the main passage for the tea-horse mutual trade. This Route starts in Guanzhong area (present day Shaanxi Province) at the eastern end, going westwards through Qinghai, crossing the Jinsha River at the northwest corner of Sichuan, passing Qamdo and Nagqu areas in Xizang, and ends in Luoxie (present day Lhasa City).

From the time of the Five dynasties to the early years of the Song Dynasty, frequent wars over the Central Plains led to a large demand for horses from the areas inhabited by Zang people. Meanwhile, in order to strengthen ties with tribes there

为使边贸有序进行，更为了维系大宋王朝的权威，宋代还设有专门管理茶马交易的机构"检举茶监司"。由于当时藏族对茶叶已十分依赖，"嗜茶如命。如不得茶，非病即死"，因此茶马互市对维护宋朝在西南地区的安全与稳定起到了重要作用。

through the tea trade, an official barter trade system was established to regulate the tea-horse mutual trade. Hence exporting tea to the areas inhabited by Zang people became a national policy implemented directly by the central government. As the only passage for tea-horse mutual trade, the Ancient Tea-horse Road experienced a considerable boom and expansion.

In order to keep the border trade in an orderly manner and more importantly to maintain the dignity and authority of the Song Dynasty, the Song-dynasty government specifically instituted an agency named Office for the Administration and Inspection of Tea Trade to supervise the tea-horse mutual trade. As tea had already become a stable food for the Zang people, it was cherished by them "as if their life depends on it". Hence the tea-horse mutual trade naturally played a crucial role in safeguarding the security and stability of the southwest frontier region at that time.

- 西藏大昭寺内描绘文成公主进吐蕃的壁画
A Mural Painting in Jokhang Temple, Xizang, Depicting a Scene When Princess Wencheng was Welcomed in Tubo

吐蕃与松赞干布

公元7-9世纪，藏族先民在青藏高原建立了吐蕃政权，它由松赞干布创立并延续两百多年，是西藏历史上的第一个政权。松赞干布的吐蕃王朝适应奴隶社会的需要，制定法律及职官、军事制度，统一了度量衡，创制了文字，与唐朝及天竺（今印度）、尼婆罗（今尼泊尔）广泛交往，佛教也于此时正式传入吐蕃。

Tubo Kingdom and Songtsän Gampo

Between the 7th and the 9th century, Zang people established the Tubo Kingdom on the Qinghai-Xizang Plateau. Founded by King Songtsän Gampo, this regime was the first of its kind in history of Xizang and lasted for more than two hundred years. During the reign of Songtsän Gampo, the administration adapted itself to the needs of a serfdom society, instituted laws, established official posts and military systems, unified measurements and created a written language. Meanwhile, the kingdom pursued extensive communication with the governments of Tang, Tianzhu (present day India) and Niger Borneo (present day Nepal). Also it was during this period that Buddhism was officially introduced into Tubo.

- 铜镀金松赞干布像（清）

松赞干布（617-650）是吐蕃王国的创建者。

A Gold-plated Bronze Statue of Songtsän Gampo (Qing Dynasty, 1611-1911)

Songtsän Gampo (617-650), is the founder of the Tubo Kingdom.

> ## 元明清的繁荣

元代，统治中原的蒙古人并不缺少马匹，官府废止了宋代实行的茶马治边政策，边茶主要以银两和土货交易。不过元朝为了加强对藏族聚居区的治理，在茶马古道沿线建立了历史上著名的"土官治土民"的土司制度。自此茶马互市和茶马古道的管理、经营均发生了重要变化。茶马古道既是经贸之道、文化之道，又是边防之道，即中央政府的治藏、安藏之道。

明朝开国后，在"以茶驭番"思想的指导下，官营茶马贸易体制得以建立，茶马互市再度恢复。一直到清代中期，基本上沿袭了宋代的做法，清代后期才逐渐废止。1371年，朝廷最先在秦（今甘肃天

> ## Prosperity during the Yuan, Ming and Qing Dynasties

During the Yuan Dynasty, the Mongols who ruled the Central Plains had no shortage of horses. Therefore, they abolished the tea-horse mutual trade based border governance policy implemented during the preceding Song Dynasty. Border trade was conducted mainly through trading in cash and local specialties for tea. Nevertheless, for the sake of strengthened governance over the areas inhabited by Zang people, the Yuan rulers introduced a historically well-known Local Governance System in areas along the Ancient Tea-horse Road. The essence of the system was to govern the native people through native chieftains. This new measure brought about profound changes to the operation and management of the Ancient Tea-

• 骑马俑（元）
A Figurine of a Horseman (Yuan Dynasty, 1206-1368)

水)、洮（今甘肃临潭)、河（今甘肃临夏)、雅（今四川雅安）等地设了四个统管茶马交易的茶马司，把这项政策作为管理西北地区的重要手段。

明太祖朱元璋在位的洪武年间，茶马互市中的一匹上等马最

horse Road. As far as the central government was concerned, the Road had served not only economic, cultural and border defense purposes, but also as the key to govern the areas inhabited by Zang people.

Shortly after the Ming Dynasty replaced the Yuan, an official Tea-horse Trading System was established guided by the theory of Ruling the areas inhabited by Zang people through Tea and hence restored the tea-horse mutual trade. In fact, this practice initiated by the Song Administration was pretty much followed through by ensuing dynasties until mid-Qing when it was phrased out. In 1371, the central government of the Ming Dynasty, for the first time, set up four tea-horse mutual trade agencies vested with the responsibility for the administration of the tea-horse trade in Qin (present day Tianshui, Gansu Province), Tao (present day Lintan, Gansu Province), He (present day Linxia, Gansu Province) and Ya (present day Ya'an, Sichuan Province) respectively, making the policy an important tool for ruling the northwestern regions.

During the Hongwu Period (1368–1398) when Zhu Yuanzhang, Emperor Taizu of the Ming Dynasty was on the

多换120斤茶叶。而到了宣德十年（1435年），西宁、河州、洮州三地的茶马司则以1000余斤茶换取13000余匹马，合一斤茶换12匹马。明代文学家汤显祖在《茶马》一诗中写道："黑茶一何美，羌马一何殊……羌马与黄茶，胡马求金珠。"足见当时茶马交易市场的兴旺与繁荣。

由于明朝与北部蒙古人关系紧张，无法从蒙古得到军马，故只有从青藏高原获得补给。朝廷充分利用藏人嗜茶的特点，严格控制茶叶

- 明太祖朱元璋像
  A Portrait of Zhu Yuanzhang—Emperor Taizu of the Ming Dynasty

throne, the first-class horses could only be traded for at most sixty kilograms of tea in return. Later in the 10th year of the Xuande Period (1435), some thirteen thousand horses could be exchanged for merely five hundred kilograms of tea (equivalent to twenty-four horses per kilogram) at regulatory agencies in Xining, Hezhou (present day Linxia Hui Autonomous Prefecture) and Taozhou (present day Lintan County). In his poem *Tea and Horses* Tang Xianzu, a Ming Dynasty writer wrote: "What wonderful avor the black tea has, and how superb the horses raised by Qiang people are! Horses raised by Qiang people are traded for yellow tea while horses raised by northern ethnic groups are marketed for gold and pearls." This was only a glimpse of the thriving and dynamic tea-horse trade at the time.

Due to the tension with the Mongols in the north, horses for the royal army of the Ming Empire could no longer be supplied by the northern neighbors. So the Great Ming had to get its supplies from the Qinghai-Xizang Plateau. Taking advantage of Zang people's love for tea, the central government of the Ming Dynasty exerted strict control over the production, shipment and sales of tea.

的生产、运输、销售，茶叶只许换取藏马。由于不是等价交换，再加上走私活动的泛滥，以及朝贡贸易的发展、运输困难等，导致了明朝官营茶马贸易体制的衰落。

清朝初年承袭明朝旧制，于顺治二年（1645年）正式恢复和延续了茶马互市这种特殊的民族贸易形式。康熙四十一年（1702年），在打箭炉（今四川康定）设立茶关。之后，又于大渡河上建泸定桥，开辟直达打箭炉的交通要道。打箭炉成为川茶输藏的集散地和川藏茶马大道的交通枢纽。康熙五十七年

- 藏族錾花双龙戏珠纹铜马鞍前桥（清）
A Zang-style Bronze Pommel Carved with the Pattern of Two Loongs Frolicking with a Pearl (Qing Dynasty, 1616-1911)

Tea was only allowed to barter for horses. Due to unfair trading terms, rampant smuggling as well as the growing tributary trade and the difficulties of transportation, the official Tea-horse Trading System eventually declined during the Ming Dynasty.

Tea-horse mutual trade continued in the early years of the Qing Dynasty, and this particular form of trade was officially resumed by the central government of the Qing Dynasty in the second year of the reign of Emperor Shunzhi (1645). In the 41st year of the reign of Emperor Kangxi (1702), the central government set up a Tea Customs at Dajianlu (present day Kangding or Darzêdo, Sichuan Province). Later, the Luding Bridge was built across the Dadu River, opening a direct access to Dajianlu where merchants gathered to ship tea from Sichuan Province to Xizang. Dajianlu was therefore made the base for tea to Xizang and an essential hub on the Tea-horse Road. In the 57th year of the reign of Emperor Kangxi (1718), to put down the riot in Junggar, the Qing-dynasty government opened up the southern Sichuan-Xizang Route, which starts from Dajianlu, going through Litang and Batang of Sichuan, Jiangka of Xizang (present day Mangkang), Chaya

（1718年），清廷为平定准噶尔叛乱，又开辟了自打箭炉经四川理塘、巴塘，西藏江卡（今芒康）、察雅至昌都的川藏南路大道。由于这条路主要供驻藏官兵来往以及运输进藏粮饷，故习惯称为"川藏官道"，实际上此道也经常是茶商驮队行经之路。而由打箭炉经四川道孚、甘孜、德格，西藏江达至昌都的茶马古道，则习惯上被称为"川藏商道"。两道会合于昌都。

to the far end in Qamdo. As this road was built mainly for the transportation of troops and military supplies between Sichuan and Xizang, it was habitually referred to as the "Sichuan-Xizang Official Route". Of course, tea caravans often made good use of the road as well. Meanwhile, the Ancient Tea-horse Road from Dajianlu, through Daofu, Ganzi and Dege of Sichuan and Jiangda of Xizang, to Qamdo was referred to as the "Sichuan-Xizang Commercial Route". Both routes converge at Qamdo.

● 清代骑兵
Cavalry Man of the Qing Dynasty

> 近现代的盛衰

虽然在清雍正十三年（1735年），官营茶马交易制度被终止，但清末民初时茶商大增，茶马古道依然繁荣。除藏族商人外，还有许多汉族、纳西族的商人。他们或雇请人背运，或用马帮、牦牛驮运，将茶叶、食盐、布匹等运进藏族聚居区，再将藏族聚居区的兽皮、药材等土特产品运往川、滇两省，往返于茶马古道之上。

抗日战争期间，日本军队阻断了所有入华通道，尤其是在缅甸沦陷、滇缅公路被切断后，滇藏线的茶马古道成为重要的国际通道。许多国外援华物资，以及内地运往滇西前线的抗战物资，都是通过这条古道由马帮运送。当时在滇缅边境

> Rise and Fall in Modern and Contemporary Times

Although the official Tea-horse Trading System was terminated in the 13th year of the reign of Emperor Yongzheng of the Qing Dynasty (1735), the Ancient Tea-horse Road remained busy and prosperous during the late years of the Qing Dynasty and the early years of the Minguo Period, and witnessed a notable increase of tea merchants. In addition to Zang people, the Han people and Naxi people also joined the ranks of merchants, shuttling between Sichuan, Yunnan and the areas inhabited by Zang people on the Ancient Tea-horse Road. They used any means necessary such as native porters, horse troops or yaks for transportation, bringing tea, salt and cloth into the areas inhabited by Zang people and shipping back local products such as furs and herbs.

参加抗战的中国军人达16万之多，加上抗日游击队，总人数达20万以上。他们绝大部分的日常供给和枪支弹药都是由滇西各族马帮经过茶马古道运送的。在中华民族生死存亡之际，茶马古道这条古老的贸易通道发挥了重要的作用，在历史上留下了它光彩的一笔。

用茶马交易来治边的制度从唐代始，至清代止，历经岁月沧桑逾

- 20世纪40年代茶马古道上的商队
A Merchant Caravan on the Ancient Tea-horse Road in the 1940s

During the War of Resistance against Japanese Invasion, the Japanese invaders almost blocked all international access to China. In particular, after the fall of Myanmar, the Myanmar-Yunnan highway was completely cut off, leaving the Ancient Yunnan-Xizang Tea-horse Road the artery of international access to China. Large quantities of international aid and domestic supplies to western Yunnan frontiers were shipped through this ancient road by caravans. On the borders between Myanmar and Yunnan, more than 160,000 Chinese army soldiers fought in battles against the Japanese invaders, alongside some 40,000 local guerillas. Most of their daily necessities, firearms and ammunitions were delivered by local caravans via this ancient road. Indeed the Ancient Tea-horse Road played a vital role in China's resistance against the Japanese invasion when the destiny of the Chinese nation was at stake. This was a glorious closing note to the history of the Ancient Tea-horse Road.

The border-governing system for tea-horse mutual trade emerged in the Tang Dynasty and died out in late Qing Dynasty, witnessing nearly one thousand years of vicissitudes. Today with the suspension of the tea-horse mutual trade, the Ancient Tea-horse Road has become

千年。现在茶马互市早已终止，古道丧失了昔日的作用。然而，茶马古道作为中华民族形成过程中的一个历史见证，依然熠熠生辉，并随着时间的流逝而日益凸显其历史意义和价值。茶马古道的国际意义堪比丝绸之路，同样亘古数千载，至今已可称之为重要的人类历史文化遗产。

redundant. The Road, as a historical witness to the evolution of the Chinese nation, still shines with glamour and will increasingly display its historical significance and value with the passing of time. The international significance of the Ancient Tea-horse Road enjoys the same reputation as that of the Ancient Silk Road, which also dates back for thousands of years. Both of them could be regarded as important historical and cultural heritage of mankind.

最早探寻茶马古道的外国人

1899年，42岁的法国人方苏雅（Auguste Francois，1857—1935）任驻云南府（今昆明）名誉总领事兼法国驻云南铁路委员会代表。他带着相机抵达昆明，开始涉足险峻难行的茶马古道。在此后的将近5年时间里，他还由昆明经楚雄，从元谋沿金沙江而上，进入四川的人小凉山，穿过泸定桥全康定，冉至川藏交界处，拍摄了许多关于沿途见闻、当地的彝族和藏族风情，以及人背马驮运送茶叶的照片，写了大批日记。他最早记录并向世界披露了茶马古道的重要特征，使这条古道受到了国际关注。

The First Foreigner Who Explored the Ancient Tea-horse Road

In 1899, 42-year-old Frenchman Auguste Francois (1857–1935) was appointed the Honorary Consul General of France to the Capital City of Yunnan Prefecture (present day Kunming City) concurrent the Representative of the French Railway Commission in Yunnan. He arrived in Kunming with his camera, and went on an adventurous expedition along the Ancient Tea-horse Road. In nearly five years, he completed an extraordinary journey through Kunming, Chuxiong,

Yuanmou, along the Jinsha River into Liangshan areas in Sichuan Province, passing the Luding Bridge to Kangding. Eventually he arrived at the border between Sichuan Province and Xizang Autonomous Region. He took many pictures of local Zang and Yi people, as well as some porters and horses of tea caravans along the way. He also kept piles of diaries documenting and revealing to the world some distinct features of this antient road for the first time, which attracted much attention from the international community.

- 方苏雅（左）与当时广西提督苏元春合影
  Auguste Francois (Left) and Su Yuanchun, Then Governor of Guangxi

- 方苏雅拍摄的运茶马队照片
  A Tea Caravan, Taken by Auguste Francois

古道寻踪
Traces of the Ancient Tea-horse Road

所谓茶马古道，并非指唯一的某一条大道，而是指以藏、滇、川交界处的"三角地带"为中心，跨越横断山脉和喜马拉雅山脉的诸多道路。在交织密布的道路网中，有两条主要的大道，它们就是著名的"滇藏道""川藏道"。而在茶马古道上将茶叶、马匹、皮毛、藏药往来运输的，就是脚夫和大大小小的马帮。

The so-called Ancient Tea-horse Road refers to not just one single road, instead it is the generic term for many pathways in the "Triangle Region" across the Hengduan Mountains and the Himalayas where Xizang Autonomous Region, Sichuan and Yunnan provinces meet. Among such an intertwined traffic network, there existed two major well-known routes, namely the Yunnan-Xizang Route and the Sichuan-Xizang Route. It was porters and caravans big and small that carried tea, horses, furs and medicine between destinations on this ancient road.

> 茶马古道之滇藏道

滇藏道的主要路线是从今天云南省的普洱市等主要产茶区向北，经丽江、香格里拉、德钦进入西藏的芒康；再从芒康向西经左贡，或向北经察雅，终点都是到西藏的昌都；然后再从昌都将茶叶等货物运到终点拉萨。

滇藏道是"滇茶藏销、藏马滇销"的主干线，形成于唐代，其历史比川藏道更为悠久。历史上由于受交通条件的限制，故只能在陆地上利用大批马帮和脚夫从云南把茶叶运到西藏，然后就地贸易或再转往印度和尼泊尔等地。马帮除了把茶叶、盐等从云南运到西藏外，还从西藏购买特产或直接买藏马回云南销售。

> Yunnan-Xizang Route of the Ancient Tea-horse Road

The Yunnan-Xizang Route starts from the present-day Pu'er City or other major tea-growing areas in Yunnan Province. It goes westwards and passes by Lijiang, Zhongdian (present-day Shapri-la county) and Deqin, enters Xizang at Mangkang, then goes further westwards by way of Zogang, or northwards by way of Chaya to Qamdo before reaching Lhasa—the most common destination.

As the transportation artery for tea from Yunnan to Xizang and horses to Yunnan, the Yunnan-Xizang Route can trace its origin back to the Tang Dynasty and has a history even longer than that of the Sichuan-Xizang Route. Due to extremely rough road conditions, ancient merchants had to rely on caravans and

滇藏道的大部分位于青藏高原上，途中经过无数大小雪山，海拔都在3000—5000米。途中经过横断山脉、金沙江、澜沧江等地，更艰难的是青藏高原上无数的冰峰雪岭。

商队通常是在每年5月雨季到来之前通过云南西南部地区，这是由于云南的雨季气候湿热，瘟疫等疾病流行，人和骡马都极易染病。滇

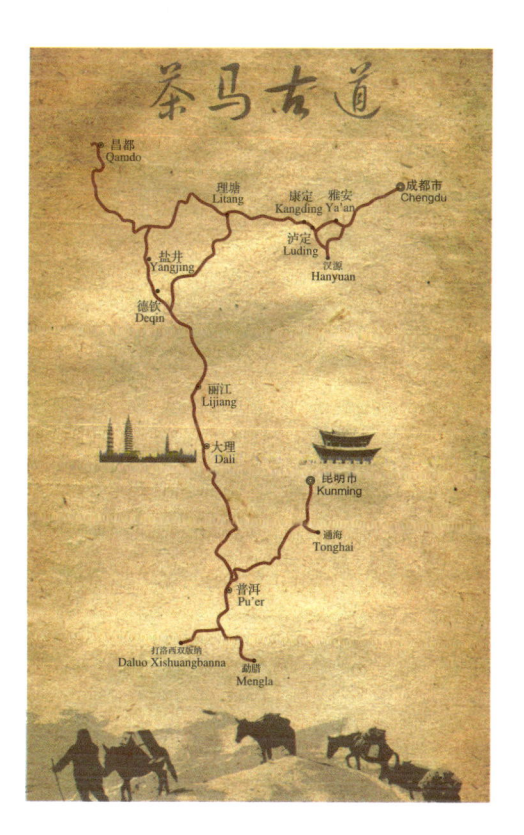

porters to carry tea from Yunnan to Xizang before shipping it further to India and Nepal. While these caravans shipped tea, salt and other commodities from Yunnan to Xizang, they also brought back horses and other local specialties.

The Yunnan-Xizang Route runs mostly on the Qinghai-Xizang Plateau and makes its way over many snow-covered mountains at the elevation of 3,000-5,000 meters. It goes through many dangerous areas in the Hengduan Mountains, along the Jinsha and the Lancang rivers, and particularly those ice-peaks and snow-mountains on the Qinghai-Xizang Plateau where the challenges are tremendous.

Usually, caravans must pass southwestern Yunnan before the rainy season begins in May. For in Yunnan, the hot and humid weather during the rainy season might easily bring about plague and other epidemics infecting both humans and animals. And it was a hard way to travel to Xizang by way of northwestern Yunnan where leeches were rampant in the summer and snow was heavy in the winter. Even

- 茶马古道示意图
  Sketch Map of Ancient Tea-horse Road

滇藏茶马古道上的梓里桥

梓里桥又名"金龙桥",位于云南省丽江市永胜县和古城区之间的金沙江上,建于清光绪六年(1880),是长江上现存最古老的桥梁。桥的主体结构是由16根大铁链悬系在两岸,上铺横竖两层木板,长116米,桥面宽3米,是中国现存桥面最宽、铁索最多的铁索桥。

Zili Bridge on the Yunnan-Xizang Route

Completed in the 6th year of the reign of Emperor Guangxu of the Qing Dynasty (1880) linking between Yongsheng County and the old town of Lijiang, Yunnan Province, the Zili Bridge, also known as the "Golden Loong Bridge" over the Jinsha River is the oldest bridge on the Yangtze River. It is comprised of 16 huge iron chains fixed on pillars on both side of river, upon which paved double layers of planks (one being arranged horizontally and the other crosswise). 116 meters long and three meters wide, this chain bridge is the widest of its kind and has the most numbers of chains among existing chain bridges in China.

西北和西藏地区,夏有蚂蟥之害,冬有大雪封山,行走异常艰难。即使在天气好时,马帮驮队也步履维艰,有的通道极为狭窄,宽不及尺,一边是绝壁,一边是深渊。再加上路途遥远,沿途缺乏供给,人马容易困乏,因而常出现人亡马死事故。

when the weather was fine, porters and caravans had to struggle on the way as the trails were extremely narrow — no wider than a foot — and were on steep cliffs above deep canyons. Moreover, travelers and horses easily got fatigued from such a long journey and from lack of supplies along the way. As a result, fatal accidents of men and horses often occurred.

虽然路途艰险，但滇藏道沿途的风景十分壮观。历史文化名城大理、丽江，风光秀丽神奇的香格里拉，雄伟壮丽的雪山群，幽深险峻的大峡谷，还有神秘的宗教文化和绚丽的民族风情等，都给滇藏道增添了无数壮丽的风景。

- 玉龙雪山

玉龙雪山位于云南省丽江西北，由13座山峰组成，由北向南呈纵向排列，延绵近50千米，不仅气势磅礴，而且秀丽挺拔，造型玲珑，在蓝天映衬下，像一条玉龙在飞舞。在当地纳西族和其他民族心目中，玉龙雪山是一座神圣的山。

The Jade Loong Snow Mountain

The Jade Loong Snow Mountain lies northwest to Lijiang, Yunnan Province and has 13 peaks in a north-to-south longitudinal arrangement, stretching out nearly 50,000 meters. Foregrounding the fine and imposing features against the blue sky the mountain looks like a flying jade loong. It is a sacred mountain in the eyes of local Naxi and other ethnic groups.

In spite of the dangerous road conditions, the Yunnan-Xizang Route offered a spectacular view along the way. Travelers may stop by Dali and Lijiang — two well-known cities for their long history and rich culture, and enjoy the great landscapes in the beautiful Shangri-La, magnificent snow-capped mountains, grand valleys and canyons, and experience the mysterious religious culture and a variety of ethnic customs. All these added numerous fascinating elements to the Yunnan-Xizang Route.

> 茶马古道之川藏道

川藏道以今天的四川雅安一带产茶区为起点，首先进入康定；自康定起，川藏道又分成南、北两条支线：北线是从康定向北，经道孚、炉霍、甘孜、德格和西藏的江达抵达昌都，再由昌都通往卫藏地区（西藏的拉萨、山南、日喀则等地区）；南线则是从康定向南，经雅江、理塘、巴塘和西藏的芒康、左贡至昌都，再由昌都通向卫藏地区。

在唐代，西藏地区与中原往来的主要通道是青藏道，即由关中地区沿河西走廊经过今天甘肃的兰州和青海的西宁、玉树，再经西藏昌都、那曲直至拉萨，这也是当时茶马互市贸易的主道。到了宋代，随

> Sichuan-Xizang Route of the Ancient Tea-horse Road

The Sichuan-Xizang Route starts from the present-day Ya'an, Sichuan Province, a tea-growing area, and bifurcates at Kangding in two directions: the north line goes northwards, passing by Daofu, Luhuo, Ganzi and Derge, entering Xizang by way of Jiangda, and arriving in Qamdo before going further to the Weizang area (Lhasa, Shannan, Shigatse, etc.); whereas the south line goes southwards, passing by Yajiang, Litang and Batang, entering Xizang by way of Mangkang and Zogang, and arriving in Qamdo before going further to the Weizang area.

During the Tang Dynasty, people travelled between Xizang and the Central Plains mainly via the Qinghai-Xizang passage, which was also the main passage

藏族茶具
A Tea Set of Zang People

着吐蕃王朝的瓦解，青藏道失去了军事要道和官道的作用，北宋在四川设置茶马司，青藏道由军事要道变为茶道。

而川藏道是从明代开始正式形成，随着茶叶贸易的开拓和发展逐渐取代了青藏道的地位。清朝进一步加强了对藏族聚居区的管理，放宽茶叶输藏政策，打箭炉成为南路边茶总汇之地，促进了川藏道的繁荣。

由于川藏道崎岖难行，由雅安运至康定的茶叶，仅少部分靠骡马驮运，大部分则要靠人力搬运。从康定到拉萨，要经过很多人迹罕至

for the Tea-horse mutual trade. The Qinghai-Xizang Route starts from the Guanzhong area, going westwards along the Hexi Corridor (to the west of the Yellow River), passing the present day Lanzhou of Gansu, Xining and Yushu of Qinghai, and enters Xizang by way of Qamdo and Nagqu before arriving in Lhasa. Coming to the Song Dynasty, this once official road and military artery lost its military significance along with the collapse of the ancient Tubo Kingdom. During the Northern Song Dynasty, the government set up a regulatory agency in Sichuan to govern the tea-horse mutual trade. Since then, the road began to serve as route for tea-trade instead of military purposes.

The Sichuan-Xizang Route was officially started during the Ming Dynasty. Along with the development of the tea trade, it gradually replaced the Qinghai-Xizang Route. The Qing-dynasty government strengthened its administration of the areas inhabited by Zang people and exerted less control over the export of tea to Xizang. Dajianlu on

的草原和茂密的森林，渡过奔腾咆哮的大河，爬过巍峨的雪峰。马帮在通过狭窄的山路前，会以铃声、锣声或以"赶马调"的歌声"鸣笛"，通知前方，以防拥堵"撞车"。万一在狭窄陡峭的岩壁前两

the south line became the hub of tea trade in the border area, which benefited the prosperity of the Sichuan-Xizang Route.

As the road conditions were very rough along the Sichuan-Xizang Route, traders had to rely mainly on porters rather than horses and mules, to carry the

- 川藏茶马古道上的藏式伸臂桥

伸臂桥是藏族聚居区特有的一种木桥，两岸百姓各自就地取材，选择河岸较窄之处，用石块在岸边砌筑桥墩，用4—6根圆木平排并列，一端砌置桥墩，一端向河心伸展，渐次撑拱，形成两岸悬臂，最后架上圆木为梁，梁上再铺木板为桥面，有的还装上木制栏杆。伸臂桥不用一铁一钉，已成为藏族聚居区的一道独特景观。

A Zang Style Overhanging Bridge on the Sichuan-Xizang Route

A Zang style overhanging bridge is a kind of wooden bridge only found in the areas inhabited by Zang people. To build such a bridge, people living along the river have to collect the best materials available such as stones and logs. They first put up stone piers on a narrow spot on the bank, place four to six logs side by side and fix them to a pier horizontally, with one end fastened to the pier and the other extending to the center of the river. Then they place logs layer by layer to form an arch—this support structure is like two arms reaching out to each other across the river, and finally complete the bridge with logs as bridge deck and planks for pavement. Some even have wooden railings. The beauty of such a bridge is that not a single iron nail is used during construction. Today, such bridges have become a part of the unique landscapes of Xizang.

队马帮相遇，进退无路，只能双方协商作价，将瘦弱的马匹推下万丈悬崖，以便让对方马匹通过。在长途运输中，高原地区天寒地冻，气候变化莫测，每日行程仅有20—30里，川藏茶马古道就是在这样的环境中开拓出来的。

tea from Ya'an to Kangding. On the way from Kangding to Lhasa, they had to pass through inaccessible grasslands, dense forests, roaring rivers, and towering snow peaks. Reaching a narrow mountain trail, caravans had to ring a bell, strike a gong or sing a horsemen's song loudly, to notify any other caravans coming the other way that they were coming, in order to prevent collision of two caravans going in opposite directions. When two caravans met on a path of a deep cliff that was too narrow to pass abreast, the parties would engage in a tough negotiation and bargain. Based on agreed prices, weaker horses would be sacrificed and pushed down the cliff, in order to make room for other horses to pass through. Moreover, the freezing temperature and unpredictable weather conditions on the plateau made it extremely hard for caravans to travel fast. On average, caravans could only advance about 10-15 kilometers in a day. It was in such adverse conditions that ancient traders and caravans treaded the Sichuan-Xizang Route.

- 茶马古道上的马蹄印
  Hoof Prints on the Ancient Tea-horse Road

> 马帮与脚夫

茶马古道上汇集着各民族的赶马人,他们长途跋涉,风餐露宿,演绎着浪漫的传奇人生。

古道上的马帮

马帮在云南历史上是一种独特的地方文化形态。马帮的发展与茶马古道的兴盛紧密联系在一起,马帮为西南地区的对外贸易提供了便利,茶马古道的繁荣则促进了马帮运输业的扩展。云南在历史上以产马著称。考古学家从170万年前元谋人时期的哺乳动物化石中就发现了马的化石;汉唐时期,云南有著名的"越賧马";宋代的"大理马"更是驰名于世。

马帮形成初期,各家各户只将

> Caravans and Porters

On the Ancient Tea-horse Road, horsemen of different ethnic backgrounds travelled long distance, spent nights in wilderness. Many left legendary stories about their lives on the Ancient Tea-horse Road.

Caravans on the Ancient Road

Historically, caravans were a unique local cultural phenomenon in Yunnan. The emergence of caravans was closely tied to the prosperity of the Ancient Tea-horse Road. Caravans helped facilitate trade and communication between the southwest China and the outside world; and the prosperity of this ancient road contributed to the booming of the caravan business. Yunnan is known for quality horses. Archaeologists have found fossils of horses among mammal

自己的马匹用于短途驮运。随着对外贸易的发展，需要进行长途贩运的货物逐渐增多，加之复杂的道路状况，单人匹马很难成行，也无力承担全部运输业务，于是便数人相约合伙同行，共运一批货物，从而形成了最初的马帮。

云南马帮的组织形式有三种。第一种是家族式的，全家人都投入马帮事业，骡马全为自家所有，且以自家的姓氏命名。第二种是"逗凑帮"，一般是同一村子或相近村

fossils some 1.7 million years ago during the time of the Yuanmou Man. There were also famous local breed as Yuedan during the Han and Tang dynasties and the more prestigious Dali breed during the Song Dynasty.

During early years of the caravans, local people only used their own horses to carry commodities to nearby destinations. With the expansion of export trade, the need for long-distance commodity transportation increased significantly. Faced with such a growing

• 马帮常用的马铃、马鞍等马具
Bells, Saddles, and Harnesses Commonly Used by a Caravan

• 行走在茶马古道上的马帮
今天，大多数地区的运输都以汽车代替了驮马，但在云南的一些边远山区，马匹至今仍是重要的交通运输工具之一。

A Caravan on the Ancient Tea-horse Road
Today, motor vehicles have replaced packhorses as means of transportation in most parts of Yunnan Province. However, in some remote mountainous areas, caravans remain one of the major means of transportation.

子的人，每家出几匹骡马，结队而行，各自照看自家的骡马，选一个德高望重、经验丰富的人做"马锅头"。马锅头负责马帮各种采买、开销、联系以及决策，不但是运输活动的直接参与者和经营者，还是赶马人的雇主。他与众多赶马人同吃一锅饭时，要由马锅头掌勺分饭分菜，"锅头"的名称便由此而来。第三种为临时结帮，无固定组织，只因走同一条路，或接受同一

demand and the reality of the rough road conditions, people found it difficult to singlehandedly carry all the commodities with their own horses. So they pooled their horses together and formed partnerships to undertake the shipment of commodity. That was the earliest form of the caravan business.

In Yunnan, caravans used to be organized in three different models: model one is a family business where the whole family is engaged. The family

- 江边狭窄的马道
  A Narrow Riverside Pathway for Caravans

宗业务，或是因为担心匪患而走到一起。这三种组织形式有时会混合在一起，成为复杂而有趣的马帮景观。而进藏的马帮一般都是家族大商号的马帮。

进藏的马帮一般找滇藏边沿

马帮走过的石板路
A Stone Road Caravans Once Treaded Across

owns all the packhorses and mules, and the caravan is usually named after the family's surname; model two is a partnership between several families, usually from the same village or neighboring villages. They would pool their packhorses and mules but take care of their own animals respectively while traveling. A respected and experienced horseman is elected as the Chief of the caravan, who is in charge of accounts, procurement, business contacts and decision-making. The Chief is not only the business partner, but also other horsemen's employer. During meals, he would distribute food for other horsemen, hence nick named the Head Wok; the third model is an ad hoc arrangement between caravan members. They come together either because they are on the same route, or on the same consignment, or simply because of their fear for robberies on the way if traveling alone. Sometimes, caravans of different organizational arrangements co-exist organically in the same convoy. Generally speaking, caravans are employed by large family businesses.

Caravans going to Xizang usually hire locals living along the Yunnan-Xizang border area as horsemen and

的藏族人做赶马人，这样不会有语言和习俗的障碍。赶马人多出身贫寒，因为走茶马道不仅艰苦异常，而且还十分危险，他们为生计所迫才走上赶马的路。

guides, partially to avoid language and custom barriers. Most of the horsemen come from impoverished families and choose this hard and dangerous job only to earn a living.

- **古道上昔日的马店**

茶马古道上的城镇里的各种店铺中几乎都设有马店，一般是前面临街临仓的房子做商铺，后面的院子做马店，即前铺后店。店铺建筑形式多为两层楼房，楼下经商，楼上堆物。前铺紧依后店，多为两进院落。院内有客房、货房和马厩等，可供行商住宿和马帮歇息、存货。

An Old Horsemen's Inn on the Ancient Road

In every town on the Ancient Tea-horse Road, there are many stores, providing caravans with accommodation, storage space and other services. This kind of store-cum-inn is mostly in a two-storeyed building, serving customers on the ground floor and making use of the second floor as storage space. The inn is in the back yard (there are usually two courtyards on such premises) where there are, among others, guest rooms, storehouses, and a stable.

马帮的规矩

马帮长年累月在外奔波,环境险恶,天灾人祸随时都有可能降临。为了求得平安,马帮中除了立规矩,还产生了种种行为与语言禁忌。

马帮每事必卜。如出行日期、走向、做什么生意、能否发财,甚至吃饭、睡觉都要占卜。马帮看重出行日期,出行前要择吉日,临行前还要占卜凶吉。

马帮在途中吃饭遇到生人应邀请同餐;遇到飞禽走兽应抛食喂饲;饭前忌敲打空碗;吃饭忌坐门槛或马鞍。饭后洗碗也有规矩,最先吃完的人只洗自己的筷子,最后吃完的人要洗所有的碗筷和锅。这些规矩无论是赶马人还是同路旅行客人,都必须遵守。凡是不小心触犯了以上忌讳,就要受罚,严重的甚至会被逐出马帮。

- **古谙边的玛尼堆**
在西藏各地的山间、路口、湖边、江畔,几乎都可以看到一座座石块垒成的祭坛——玛尼堆,也称为"神堆"。

A Pile of Marnyi Stones by the Ancient Road
In Xizang, piles of Marnyi stones (also known as God's piles) —altars made of piled stones, can be found everywhere in mountains, at crossroads, by lakes and rivers.

Caravans' Rules

Long out on the move in a dangerous world, caravan members are constantly exposed to dangers natural and man-made. For the security of human lives and the commodity they carry, caravans have their own taboos against certain behaviors and languages in addition to strict operational rules.

Caravan members practice divination in every decision they make, such as when to depart, which direction to go, what kind of business to do, the odds of making a profit even what to eat and when to sleep. They believe a good start would bring good luck to the journey and therefore would carefully choose an auspicious day for departure.

- 翻越雪山的马帮
A Caravan Crossing a Snow Mountain

When they stop to have a meal, caravan members would invite strangers on the way to join them and feed birds and animals nearby. Members must not tap on an empty bowl before meals and not sit on a threshold or saddle during meals. There are also rules on dish washing: the first one finishing his meal washes his own chopsticks only while the last one washes all the other dishes and woks. These rules apply to travel companions as well as horsemen. Anyone who inadvertently violates the above-mentioned rules or taboos would face penalty. In a severe case, the violator could be expelled from the caravan.

古道上的脚夫

20世纪中叶以前，川藏线中雅安到打箭炉（今康定）一段，由于道路艰险，骡马难以通行，主要是依靠人力脚夫运茶。背茶包的脚夫长年累月地艰难攀行，遇到陡险地势，只有手脚并用，方能攀援通行。当地人俗称脚夫为"背二哥"或"背背子"。

背二哥与亲戚朋友结伴而行，一二十个为"一朋"。亲友关系便于彼此相互照应，克服困难，有难同当。一朋人中不乏父子同道，祖孙三代同行。他们选年高有德者，或久跑江湖并懂外事者为"掌拐师"，或称

Porters on the Ancient Tea-horse Road

Prior to the mid-20th century, it was porters who carried tea between Ya'an and Dajianlu (present day Kangding) on the Sichuan-Xizang Route, where road conditions were so rough that even packhorses and mules could not pass. For years, tea-carrying porters struggled yet soldiered on. When the terrain was impassable, they somehow found a way with both hands and feet. They were referred to by the local people as Porter Brothers.

Porter Brothers were virtually kin relatives and friends, doing business in a group that consisted of ten to twenty members. Such relationships forged a

●昔日茶马古道上的脚夫 (图片提供：FOTOE)
Porters on the Ancient Tea-horse Road

"拐子师" "大背师"。

脚夫从茶商的库房里领取茶包，背往指定的地方。体力好的每趟可取20—25包，足有300—400斤重。他们将领到的茶包层叠摆好，用竹签串联固定，再以篾条编成背笼套在双肩。他们手里挂着一根丁字形的拐杖，拐尖镶有铁杵，俗称"拐笆子""墩拐子"。茶包一旦上背，沿途一般不得卸下歇息。爬山途中遇有平缓处，领头的掌拐师便会审视路段和脚夫负力情形，需歇气时嘘一声口哨，用拐子在地上杵三下，示意大家找地方歇息，调整呼吸。脚夫们依

bond among the members: they took care of each other and dealt with problems together. One may find father and sons, and even three generations in the same group. A respected, older member or someone who had been long in the business and knew it well would be elected as the master.

Porters picked up tea packages from the merchant's warehouse and carried them to designated places. An able-bodied porter could pick up at a time 20-25 packages, weighing 150-200 kilograms on aggregate. They stacked up the packages, fastened them with bamboo sticks, put them in a bamboo basket and carried the basket on their shoulders. Each porter had a T-shaped pole, with an iron rod on one end. In general, porters did not take the baskets off their shoulders when they traveled. When they reached a gentle slope, the master would make a whistle and knock on the ground three times with his pole, signifying the porters to take a break and catch breath. The message would be passed down from one to the other. Group members would line up, poke their poles into the ground, and use it to support their baskets and release the burden for a moment.

Members in a group were trained to

次传递信息，一朋人一字排开，将拐杖戳在地上，用拐杖支撑起背上的茶包，以便放松肩上的肌肉，挺直腰背歇脚片刻。

由于一朋人动作训练有素，较为协调，间隔距离较整齐，即上坡70步，下坡80步，平路110步。日久天长，古道上便按照这样的距离留下了拐尖铁杵扎下的痕迹。

从雅安到打箭炉要翻越二郎山，路途十分艰险。身背几百斤茶包的背二哥要徒步而行，其艰苦程度可想而知。他们的装备极其简单。胸前系着一个椭圆形的小篾圈，俗称"汗刮子"，专用于刮

coordinate their steps with their mates while keeping a certain distance from each other. Generally, two mates would keep 70 steps apart going uphill, 80 steps downhill, and 110 steps on a level path. As porters travelled in this array for ages, they left on the ancient trails marks of iron-poles at such intervals.

The lofty Erlang Mountain on the way from Ya'an to Dajianlu (present day Kangding) made the journey very hard and dangerous for porters carrying heavy loads. One can imagine how difficult it must have been every step they took. Porters had minimal personal equipments and supplies, which included food (corn flour and a small bag of salt); a sweat scraper— an oval-shaped ring made of a slim bamboo splint to help wipe off sweat; and a pair of foot fixers — anti-slippery device made of straw or hemp ropes to help move forward on an icy road.

Liu Manqing, one of the Chinese scholars who visited Xizang during the Minguo Period, noted that: "Despite

- 古道上脚夫留下的"拐子窝"
  Marks of Porters' Poles on the Ancient Tea-horse Road

汗；自备食物，即玉米面和一小袋盐巴；冬天冰天雪地，道路很滑，必须穿"脚码子"（套在鞋上的防滑装置，多用草绳、麻绳等做成）才能平稳行走。

民国时期入藏考察的学者刘曼卿称："自雅至炉则万山丛胜，行旅甚难，沿途负茶包者络绎不绝，茶一包重约二十斤，壮者可负十三四包，老弱则仅四五包已足。肩荷者甚吃苦，行数武必一歇，尽日仅得二三十里。"

such a challenging travel from Ya'an to Dajianlu where numerous mountains lie on the way, tea-carrying porters crowded the pathway. Generally speaking, a package weighs about 10 kilograms; an able-bodied porter could carry thirteen or fourteen packages at one time while an elderly or weak one no more than four or five packages. It was a very hard job. Porters had to stop and catch their breath every few steps. So they could only travel 10-15 kilometers a day."

- 茶马古道上的廊桥
A Covered Bridge on the Ancient Tea-horse Road

古道集市寺登街

　　大理剑川县南部的沙溪镇是茶马古道的要冲，镇内的寺登街更是以古道上唯一幸存的集市而闻名。据地方史料记载，沙溪寺登街形成于元末明初，明代即已初具规模，清末至民国是其鼎盛时期。寺登街的崛起与云南马帮的兴起有很大的关系。有人说"寺登街是马帮用马驮出来的"。在鼎盛时期，寺登街每隔三天就有一个街市。届时，马帮交会，商贾云集，有买有卖，热闹非凡。寺登街上的铁匠铺不少，与别处的铁匠铺不同，这里铁匠铺的主要业务是打马钉、马掌，供马帮使用。今日

- **沙溪寺登街的古戏台**
  An Ancient Stage on Sideng Street, Shaxi Town

这座古戏台建于清光绪四年（1878年），第一层为戏台，其上为亭阁，古戏台的木雕与建筑形式都具有鲜明的大理风格。古戏台是古镇的文艺活动中心，每到赶庙会的日子，人们就要在这里搭台唱戏，热闹一番。

Completed in the 4th year during the reign of Emperor Guangxu of the Qing Dynasty (1878), this ancient stage has a plantform on the ground level and pavilions above. One may find distinctive local artistic features of Dali in the wood carvings and the overall architecture. The stage is a community center where locals gather to watch performances on occasions like trade fairs and festivals.

的寺登街集市街面全由条石铺成，被马蹄和人足踩得凸凹锃亮的石块，展示着历史的沧桑。千年古树、古道、古宅、古桥、古戏台、魁阁、古寨门依然可见。2001年10月，沙溪寺登街被正式列入"2002年世界纪念性建筑遗产保护名录"。

Sideng Street Market on the Ancient Tea-horse Road

Shaxi Town in the south part of Jianchuan County, Dali Bai Autonomous Prefecture, is not only known for its fortress on the Ancient Tea-horse Road, but also for the street market of Sideng, which is the only one that survived the times. According to local historical records, the Sideng Street Market first appeared during the late Song and early Ming dynasties, and developed into a primary size market during the Ming Dynasty and reached its peak in the Qing Dynasty and the Minguo Period. The rise of the street was closely related to the rise of caravans in Yunnan. It was said that the street had been built on the horse back of caravans. During its prime time, the street accommodated a busy trade fair every three days, where caravans and merchants flooded the street from all over the place and made business transactions there. There were many blacksmith shops on the street; yet unlike in other places, these blacksmith shops mainly served caravans, by helping them make and repair horseshoes and spurs. Today, one may find that many of the square-stones on this street deformed and shiny after years of treading by horses and men. Indeed, one can perceive from these stones the vicissitudes of history. Traces of history can also be found everywhere in the street: one-thousand-year-old trees, ancient roads, houses, bridges, opera stage, tower, and entrance gate. In October 2001, Sideng Street was incorporated into the "2002 List of Monumental Architectural Heritage of the World".

古道茶香
Tea Aroma on the Ancient Tea-horse Road

中国是茶的故乡，茶是中国的国饮，上自帝王贵胄、文人名士，下至贩夫走卒，无不饮茶。茶早就成为中国人生活中不可缺少的一部分。茶马古道以茶树的发源地云南普洱、西双版纳和四川雅安为起点，茶叶理所当然是古道上最重要的货物。

China is the homeland of tea, and tea is China's national beverage. In China people of all social strata enjoy tea since ancient times. Indeed tea has become an indispensable part of the life of the Chinese people. The Ancient Tea-horse Road started in Xishuangbanna of Yunnan Province and Ya'an of Sichuan Province respectively. As both being regions where tea was first cultivated in ancient times, tea naturally became the most important merchandise on this ancient road.

> 茶马古道上的茶

茶马古道分为滇藏道和川藏道两条路线，而滇藏道上运输的主要是产于云南西双版纳六大茶山的普洱茶，川藏道上运输的则主要是产于四川雅安地区的四川边茶。

普洱茶

普洱茶产于云南省南部的普洱、西双版纳、昆明和宜良等地，是滇藏茶马古道上最重要的货物。所谓普洱茶，人们一般认为指的是以澜沧江流域的古"六大茶山"所产的大叶种茶为原料，经杀青、揉捻、晒干等工序加工而成的晒青毛茶，以及由晒青毛茶压制而成的各种规格的紧压茶。

> Tea on the Ancient Tea-horse Road

The Ancient Tea-horse Road had two major routes, i.e. the Yunnan-Xizang Route and the Sichuan-Xizang Route. While the Yunnan-Xizang Route transported mainly Pu'er Tea produced in the six well-known tea-growing mountains in Xishuangbanna of Yunnan, the Sichuan-Xizang Route carried mainly Border Tea produced in Ya'an of Sichuan.

Pu'er Tea

Pu'er Tea grows in Pu'er, Xishuangbanna, Kunming and Yiliang in Southern Yunnan. It uses the Yunnan sun-greened grandifoliage tea as the raw material, and became the most important merchandise on the Yunnan-Xizang Route. Most

• 茶叶的采摘
Tea Picking

云南是茶树的原生地，全国乃至全世界很多茶叶的根源都在这里。早在3000多年前，云南地区就已经有人种茶，并将制作的茶敬奉给周武王。而普洱茶的历史最早可以追溯到东汉时期，民间对普洱茶有"武侯遗种"之称，"武侯"是指三国时期的蜀汉丞相诸葛亮，故普洱茶的种植至少已有1700年的历史。唐朝时，普洱茶开始大规模种植，当时被人称为"普茶"。宋明时期，普洱茶向中原地带蔓延，而且在边疆和对外经济贸易中扮演

people use Pu'er Tea as a generic term, referring to sun-greened raw tea from the six well-known tea-growing mountains in the Lancang River basin, after withering, rolling and drying processes, or the various compressed tea made from the same materials.

Yunnan is the habitat of tea tree. Most tea varieties in China and even in other parts of the world could trace their origins from Yunnan. As early as 3,000 years ago, people began to grow tea in Yunnan Province and offered it as a tribute to King Wu of the Zhou Dynasty. The first written record of Pu'er Tea appeared

了很重要的角色。到了清朝，普洱茶贸易达到了鼎盛。雍正七年（1729年），清政府在普洱茶产地设置普洱府，下辖今天的普洱市和西双版纳傣族自治州，普洱茶也被正式列为贡茶。普洱茶进入清宫以后，以其浓厚独特的茶味深得帝王和皇室成员青睐。一时间，清宫中以饮普洱茶为时尚，普洱茶还常常作为国礼赠送给外国使节。清宫对普洱茶的偏好，一直延续到清朝结束。末代皇帝爱新觉罗·溥仪就曾说皇室的习惯是"夏喝龙井，冬

- 云南大叶种茶树的鲜叶
  Fresh Leaves of the Gandifoliage Tea of Yunnan Province

during the Eastern Han Dynasty. Back then, tea was referred to as the "species left by the Marquis of Wu (Prime Minister Zhuge Liang of the Kingdom Shu of the Three Kingdoms Period)". Based on this historical reference, the history of tea can be traced back to at least 1,700 years ago. Tea was widely cultivated and was known as "*Pucha* (common tea)" during the Tang Dynasty. Between the Song and the Ming dynasties, Pu'er Tea spread to the Central Plains area. At the same time, it played an important role in border trade and export trade. Later in the Qing Dynasty, Pu'er Tea witnessed its prime time. In the 7th year during the reign of Emperor Yongzheng (1729), the government set up the Pu'er Prefecture, whose jurisdiction covered the tea-producing areas including Pu'er and Xishuangbanna. Pu'er Tea was also officially listed as the tribute tea. As the Qing emperors and other members of the royal family were very fond of the unique strong aroma and texture of Pu'er Tea, it quickly became a popular drink in the Imperial Palace. Pu'er Tea was often presented to foreign envoys as a state gift. The Qing Court's love for Pu'er Tea lasted till the end of the dynasty. The last Qing emperor Puyi once said that the royal family's tea-drinking habit

喝普洱"。皇家对普洱茶的追捧，很快影响到民间，因此清代普洱茶在北京名声大振，饮用普洱茶随之在全国风行开来。

普洱茶之所以有别于其他的茶类，具有独特的风味，一个重要的原因就是在其加工中有一个"后发酵"的过程。清朝初年，每年春天，六大茶山的茶农将春天最好的茶加工后上贡皇室，然后将采摘下来的普通茶制成晒青毛茶，再经蒸

was featured by Longjing (Loong Well) Tea in the summer and Pu'er Tea in the winter. The royal family's feverish love for Pu'er Tea also influenced the common people, making such tea not only famous in Beijing, but also in other parts of the country.

What makes Pu'er Tea's unique avor is the post-fermentation process. Back in the early years of the Qing Dynasty, every spring, tea farmers in these six tea-growing mountains would pick the

- 人工压制普洱茶饼的石模
A Stone Mold Used to Manually Compress Pu'er Tea into Tea Cakes

六大茶山

　　六大茶山指出产包括普洱茶在内的云南茶叶的六大古茶山,位于西双版纳傣族自治州内。历来对六大茶山的说法很多,一般认为包括倚邦、革登、莽枝、蛮砖、曼撒和攸乐。古六大茶山的土地被各种树木、竹林、花草覆盖,终年小溪流淌,构成了一个美丽富饶的动植物王国,而且远离城镇,不受污染。这里从三国以前就开始种植茶树,明代至清代中期是普洱茶的鼎盛时期,因被朝廷列为贡茶,极大地促进了普洱茶的发展。朝廷在茶叶集散地普洱府设立了专门机构统一管理茶叶的加工制作和贸易,普洱便成为茶叶精制、进贡的中心和贸易集散地。此时,以"六大茶山"为主的西双版纳茶区,年产干茶8万担,达到了历史最高水平。清顺治十八年(1661年),仅销往西藏的普洱茶就达3万担之多。同治年间普洱茶的生产仍然兴旺,国内每年都有千余名藏族商人到此买茶,东南亚、南亚的商人也前来普洱做茶叶生意。每年有5万多匹骡、马和牛奔走在千山万水之间,马铃牛梆之声终年不绝于耳。

• 六大茶山中的曼撒茶山
Mount Mansa—One of the Six Well-Known Tea-growing Mountains

Six Well-Known Tea-growing Mountains

The six well-known tea-growing mountains refer to the six mountains where local tea (incl. Pu'er) has been growing for ages. They are all located within the Xishuangbanna Dai Autonomous Prefecture. Although there is more than one version of its constitution, it is generally believed that the mountains include, Yibang, Gedeng, Mangzhi, Manzhuan, Mansa and Youle. Green vegetation and sufficient water supply make these areas a paradise for wild life. In addition, being far away from human activities, they are free from man-made pollutions. People began to grow tea there before the Three Kingdoms Period (220–280) and expanded production of the Pu'er Tea during the Ming and mid-Qing dynasties when Pu'er Tea was designated as tribute tea to the royal family. In Pu'er Prefectur, a tea distribution center, the government set up a special agency to regulate the processing and trade in tea. This made the Pu'er Prefecture a center for tea processing, tribute tea selection, trading and distribution. At that time, the six tea-growing mountains and other tea growing areas in Xishuangbanna yielded an output of 4 million kilograms of dried tea — the highest record in history. In the 18th year during the reign of Emperor Shunzhi of the Qing Dynasty (1661), about 1.5 million kilograms of Pu'er Tea was sold to Xizang alone. During the reign of Emperor Tongzhi (1862–1874), the Pu'er Tea business remained thriving. Every year, the Prefecture attracted more than 1,000 Zang merchants, as well as businessmen from South and Southeast Asia. As caravans of more than 50,000 horses, mules and yaks travelled between mountains and rivers, one may hear horse bells and yak clappers chiming all year long.

• 倚邦茶山上的运茶马道
A Horse Road on Mount Yibang

压成形，形成形状不一的紧压茶。这种茶含水量一般较多，在运往集散地前，为防止茶叶在装筐时被挤碎，常常又要喷些清水，这样经过十天左右的路途到达目的地时，茶叶已经完成了初步的冷发酵。在集散地的茶庄，经过精心挑选，又通过马帮千里迢迢地运往藏族聚居区。这一过程又要花儿个月的时间，于是茶叶又经过了一个缓慢的冷发酵过程，最终形成了云南特有

best buds for the royal family. Then they would use the plain tea leaves to make sun-greened primary tea. The primary tea was then dried, steamed and molded into compressed tea of various shapes. In general, these compressed tea had a high moisture content. Before they were sent to the distribution center, water had to be sprinkled on the surface in order to prevent the tea cakes from being crushed when loaded into the baskets. Thus the preliminary cold fermentation process

- 普洱茶园
  A Pu'er Tea Plantation

- 普洱茶的揉捻

揉捻的目的是利用外力，使茶叶叶片揉破变轻，卷曲成条，体积缩小，使部分茶汁挤溢附在叶表，对提高茶的滋味浓度也有重要作用。传统的普洱茶揉捻都是手工操作。

The Rolling Process of Pu'er Tea

By employing external forces, rubs the tea leaves down to tiny pieces, making them lighter and curved. The process can also squeeze out some juice onto the surface of the leaves, and helping make the flavor stronger. Traditionally, Pu'er Tea is rolled manually.

- 普洱茶杀青

The Withering Process of Pu'er Tea

的后发酵茶——普洱茶。经过漫长发酵的普洱茶具有独特的陈香，而且去掉了生茶的苦涩味，茶汤柔绵醇厚，深受人们的喜爱。

人们发现这一特点后，一直

was completed in the days on the road. When these compressed tea cakes arrived at the distribution center, distributors would select the quality tea and hired caravans to ship them further to the areas inhabited by Zang people. This journey may take months and allowed for a slow cold fermentation process, which gave the tea a unique stale scent, meanwhile removing the bitter taste often found in raw unfermented tea. With its smooth and mellow taste and strong and aromatic

在探索用人工的方法，使刚生产出来的普洱茶就能像存放多年的老茶那样具有柔润滑口的风味。20世纪六七十年代，普洱茶的渥堆工艺得以推行，方法是将毛茶堆放成一定高度，洒水后上覆麻布，使之在湿热作用下发酵24小时左右，其间也有微生物参与发酵。经过渥堆后的茶叶，颜色由绿转为黄、栗红乃至栗黑，茶性变得温和，茶汤色泽金红，柔顺滑口，醇香浓郁，更适合日常饮用。渥堆发酵工艺缩短了普洱茶陈化的过程。现在一般将经过

flavor, Pu'er Tea won its popularity.

Ever since the discovery of the process, people began to explore more ways to give newly-produced tea the same smooth and mellow taste and strong aroma which was found after long fermentation. In the 1960s and 1970s, the Pile Cooking method appeared on the scene. Primary tea is piled up, sprinkled with water and covered with linen, allowing for about 24 hours of fermentation with the help of micro-organisms in a hot and humid environment. Through this process, the texture of the tea becomes milder, and the color turns from green to yellow or brownish red, sometimes dark red like the color of chestnuts. The tea water presents a golden red color with a smooth and mellow taste and strong aroma. This tea is more suitable for daily consumption. This piled fermentation method shortens the aging or fermentation process significantly. Nowadays, people call tea

- **普洱茶的晾晒**
  经过揉捻的茶叶需要置于阳光下晒干，这是茶香形成的重要过程。
  The Drying Process of Pu'er Tea
  After the rolling process, the tea leaves are sun-dried to release the aroma.

人工渥堆发酵的普洱茶称为"熟茶"，而不经过渥堆发酵而完全靠自然陈化的普洱茶称为"生茶"，其陈化转熟的过程相当缓慢，至少需要5—8年。时间越长，陈香益发醇厚和稳健。

made through the piled fermentation process the "Cooked Tea" and the naturally fermented tea the "Raw Tea". The natural aging process of the "Raw Tea" requires at least five to eight years, during which time the aroma would become stronger and the texture milder.

各种形态的普洱茶
Pu'er Tea in Various Forms

- **普洱散茶**

普洱散茶是指未经压形的普洱茶，上等的普洱散茶色泽棕褐或褐红（俗称"猪肝色"），光泽油润，陈香显露，条形肥壮完整，断碎茶少。冲泡后的茶汤红浓明亮，闻起来陈香浓郁纯正，饮一口滋味浓醇滑口，喉底回甘，舌根生津。

Bulk Pu'er Tea

Bulk Pu'er Tea is the loose tea before compression. Fine bulk tea is mostly in the form of large, complete pieces. It looks brownish or brownish-red, commonly described as the "liver-color", shiny with oil-like sheen; bringing about a stale scent and bright red, thick tea water with a strong aroma and a smooth taste. It has a sweet aftertaste and stimulates the secretion of saliva.

- 普洱饼茶

  普洱饼茶是一种外形扁平呈圆盘状的普洱紧压茶。

  Compressed Pu'er Tea Cake

  Pu'er Tea is compressed into a flat disc shape.

- 20世纪70年代中期勐海茶厂生产的七子饼茶

  七子饼茶每七块茶饼为一筒，每块净重七两，七七四十九，寓意多子多孙。在云南一些少数民族地区，儿女亲事，非送七子饼茶不可，相传至今，在旅居东南亚一带的侨胞中也很盛行这种风俗，所以，七子饼茶又名"侨销圆茶""侨销七子饼茶"。

  Seven-packed Tea Cake by Menghai Tea Company in the mid-1970s

  The Seven-packed Tea Cake usually is sold in canisters, each cake weighing 7 *Liang* (350 grams), making the total 49 *Liang*. Such numbers signify auspiciousness and fertility. In some areas inhabited by ethnic groups in Yunnan Province, the Seven-packed Tea Cake is a staple on the wedding gift list. This custom is also very popular among overseas Chinese in Southeast Asia; and such canister tea is also known as "Overseas Disk-shaped Tea" or "Overseas Seven-packed Tea Cake".

- 包装好的普洱沱茶

  Packed-up Bowl-shaped Pu'er Tea

● 普洱沱茶

普洱沱茶从上面看形似圆面包，从底下看却又中间下凹，像个厚壁碗，一般每个净重为100克或250克。在包装时，通常每五个用竹箬包成一包，以树皮绳或竹篾捆绑。据说这是为了方便古时长途运输及长期存储。

Bowl-shaped Pu'er Tea

The Bowl-shaped Pu'er Tea looks like a bagel from the top. With a concave in the middle, it looks like an upside-down thick-walled bowl. Generally speaking, each piece weighs 100 or 250 grams. Usually five such pieces would be packed into one big packet wrapped with bamboo leaves and tied up with bark laces or fine bamboo splints. It is said that such a packing method was for the convenience of long-distance transportation and long-term storage in ancient times.

● 普洱砖茶

普洱砖茶是以云南大叶茶品种为原料，精制后蒸压做形，烘干而成，长方形砖块状，每块250—1000克，成茶色泽褐红，滋味纯和，有浓郁的陈香，冲泡后的茶汤色泽红亮。

Pu'er Brick Tea

Using a local tea species known as the grandifoliage as the raw material, Pu'er Brick Tea is produced through steaming, molding and drying processes. Weighing between 250 to 1,000 grams each, the rectangular tea bricks are in a brownish red color with a pure and mild scent. The tea water is bright red, emitting a strong aroma.

051

古道茶香

Tea Aroma on the Ancient Tea-horse Road

四川边茶

"边茶"这个称呼源于明代中期,是对由四川销往藏族聚居区的茶叶的统称。在明朝,由于藏茶是涉及西藏的特殊商品,从开国皇帝朱元璋开始就形成皇帝亲自管理藏茶的习惯。明朝一般将西藏地区视为边疆,称为"边",而将朝廷直接控制的内地称为"腹"。明嘉靖年间,藏茶官商走私和民间交易盛

- 康砖茶茶样与茶汤
Sample and Tea Water Made of Kangzhuan Brick Tea

Border Tea from Sichuan

The term Border Tea first appeared during the mid-Ming Dynasty. As a generic term, it referred to all the tea sold to the areas inhabited by Zang people from Sichuan. During the Ming Dynasty, tea exported to Xizang was regarded as a special commodity bearing strategic importance to the Ming-dynasty government. Since the founding father of the Ming Dynasty, Emperor Zhu Yuanzhang who personally attended to the tea business, all his successors preserved this tradition. In general, The Ming-dynasty government regarded Xizang as the frontier while the area under the direct control of the Emperor as the heartland. During the reign of Emperor Jiajing of the Ming Dynasty, smuggling and private trading of tea to the areas inhabited by Zang people were rampant and the regulatory system existed in name only. So the government introduced a "Quota System" implemented through the Ministry of Finance of the Nanjing Government. Under the framework of the system, special tea quotas were issued for tea traded to the areas inhabited by Zang people and the heartlands respectively. Each quota allowed for the trading of 50 kilograms of tea, and taxation

• 金尖茶
Golden Tip Tea

行，明初起实行的藏茶管理制度已经名存实亡。朝廷于是改行由南京户部集权控制的"引岸制"，即由户部统一印制发行"茶引"，分为针对藏族聚居区销售的"边引"和针对内地销售的"腹引"。每引定量为100斤，朝廷按茶引收取茶税。

到了清代，各路边茶的制作形状、包装、品种都有各自的定式，并承袭下来。乾隆年间，朝廷正式将输藏的川茶称为"边茶"，分为南路边茶和西路边茶。

南路边茶产于四川雅安等地，原料粗老并包含一部分茶梗。南路边茶的成茶曾分为毛尖、芽细、康砖、金尖、金玉、金仓6个花色，后简化为康砖、金尖两个花色，品质优良，经熬耐泡，在藏族人中享有盛誉，占藏族边茶消费量的60%以上。

was collected accordingly.

Entering the Qing Dynasty, different Border Tea chose their particular sources and developed their permanent processing and packaging styles. During the reign of Emperor Qianlong, the royal administration formally named tea produced in Sichuan and sold to the areas inhabited by Zang people the "Border Tea", which was further divided into the southern route variety and the western route variety.

Southern Border Tea was made of less tender, fully-grown tea leaves including even some stalks, from Ya'an, of Sichuan and other places.

Initially, Southern Border Tea included six sub-categories: Tender Tip (Maojian), Fine Bud (Yaxi), Kang Brick (Kangzhuan), Golden Tip (Jinjian), Golden Jade (Jinyu), and Golden Warehouse (Jincang) and was later reduced to two sub-categories only, i.e. Kang Brick and Golden Tip. Because of its fine quality, durable flavor, this tea enjoyed very good reputation among the Zang people accounting for more than 60% of the total consumption of Border Tea.

Western Border Tea referred to the compressed tea made of tea leaves growing in Guanxian (present day

西路边茶简称"西边茶"，系四川灌县（今都江堰市）、北川一带生产的紧压茶，用篾包包装。以前灌县所产边茶用长方形茶包，称"方包茶"；北川所产的为圆形包，称"圆包茶"，现在圆包茶已停产，改按方包茶规格加工。西路边茶的原料比南路边茶更为粗老，产区大都实行粗细兼采制度，一般在春天采摘一次细茶之后，再采摘边茶，加工工艺比较简单，一般杀青后晒干，蒸压后装入篾包即可。西路边茶的毛茶色泽枯黄，稍带烟焦气，滋味醇和，汤色红黄，叶底黄褐。

Dujiangyan City) and Beichuan of Sichuan Province and packed in bamboo packets. People used to pack tea from Guanxian in rectangular packages and tea from Beichuan in round packages. Nowadays, the same rectangular packages have been adopted in both areas. Compared to Southern Border Tea, the raw material used to produce Western Border Tea is even more mature. Tea farmers have adopted a dual harvest practice whereby in the spring time, farmers first pick the most tender leaves by hand to make refined tea and then cut the less tender leaves to make Border Tea. The processing of the latter is also simplified into withering, drying, steaming, molding, and packaging. Western Border Tea looks scorched yellow, has a slight burning smell, and makes reddish yellow tea water with a mellow taste.

> 古道民族与茶俗

> People Living along the Ancient Tea-horse Road and Their Tea Drinking Habits

茶马古道是民族迁徙的走廊，又是各种民族文化进行交流的地区。在古道上的许多城镇中，各民族亲密和睦，多民族文化并行不悖，在交往、交流中不断交融。

The Ancient Tea-horse Road has been a passage for migration as well as a channel for cultural exchange between different ethnic groups. Multiple ethnic cultures coexist and integrate through interactions and communications.

布朗族与青竹茶

Blang People and Their Green Bamboo Tea

布朗族是一个古老的民族，主要聚居在西双版纳傣族自治州勐海县境内的布朗山。布朗族是中国古代"濮人"的后裔，早在商周时期，生活在澜沧江边云南地区的濮人就已经开始种植茶叶。

布朗人的生活与茶有着密切的联系，茶不仅用来款待贵客、馈赠亲友，而且是敬神祭祖的上佳

The Blang people whose origin can be traced back to ancient times, mostly live at Mount Blang in Menghai County, Xishuangbanna Dai Autonomous Prefecture. It is believed Blang people are descendants of the Pu people whose ancestors living by the Lancang River beginning to grow tea as early as during the Shang and Zhou dynasties.

供品。在布朗族山寨里，最常见的是烤茶，即将茶叶放在茶罐中烤制后再用开水冲泡。而当布朗族人远离家门在野外劳作时，往往会就地取材制作一种青竹茶。首先砍伐一节碗口粗的鲜竹子，一端削尖，插在地下当作煮茶容器，向竹筒中注入山泉水。然后用干枝落叶堆在竹筒四周，点燃，待水煮沸后放入茶叶，煮成茶汤，倒入短小的饮茶竹

Tea plays an important role in the life of the Blang people. They use tea to entertain distinguished guests, give tea to friends and relatives as presents, and offer tea to ancestors and divinities during worship rituals. In a Blang community, the most commonly seen tea is Roast Tea where tea is baked in a pot before adding boiling water to boil the tea. When Blang people are out in the fields, they usually make the best of what is available and make a Green Bamboo Tea through the following steps: first, they choose a fresh bamboo stem with a bowl-sized cross section; second, they sharpen one end of the bamboo and poke it into the ground vertically; third, they pour spring water into this improvised bamboo container; Fourth, they gather

● 布朗族少女
A Blang Girl

- 布朗族民居
Blang's Residence

- 布朗族的青竹茶
The Blang's Green Bamboo Tea

筒内饮用。青竹茶融合了茶香和青竹香，香醇爽口、回味无穷。

　　与青竹茶比起来，布朗族的特色菜肴"酸茶"更加风味独到。其制作法是从茶树新梢上采下茶芽，摊放在阳光下晾晒，晒到半干后用于揉搓，并与辣椒粉、花椒粉、姜末、食

dry leaves and twigs around the container and start a fire; fifth, when the water is boiling, they put in some tea leaves and brew; sixth, they pour the tea water into smaller bamboo canisters to drink. With the combined aroma of fresh bamboo and green tea, this Green Bamboo Tea has a very refreshing and lasting taste.

盐和香辛料拌匀后装进大竹筒，紧紧压实，最后用芭蕉叶密封。30天后，茶叶开始变酸，两个月后，方能开封食用。这道菜保留了茶叶被人类发现之初的食用功能，滋味甘凉浑厚，能使人胃口大开，一向是布朗族宴席上的传统佳肴。

傣族与竹筒香茶

傣族主要散居于云南省的南部和西南部地区，以西双版纳最为集中，是一个能歌善舞而又热情好客

傣族孔雀舞金刚面具
A King Kong Mask Used by the Dai People in a Peacock Dance

Compared to the Green Bamboo Tea, a local specialty dish the "Sour Tea", has a even more special taste. The preparation process is as follows: tender tea buds are picked and sun-dried; when half dry, rub them by hand and mix them with salt, chili pepper, ginger and other spices; stuff the mixture into a big bamboo bucket, press hard, and seal with banana leaves for sixty days. The tea turns sour in thirty days yet it takes sixty days to develop the desired taste. This dish kept the original function of tea as edible food. It is very tasteful and can stimulates the appetite. It has always been one of the traditional dishes in a Blang feast.

Dai People and Their Bamboo Canister-roast Tea

Dai people have been scattered in the south and southwestern Yunnan, mainly in Xishuangbanna Dai Autonomous Prefecture. They are known for their hospitality as well as their great talent for singing and dancing, In Yunnan Province, the Water Splashing Festival (Songkran Festival) is the most important festival for the Dai people as well as the most influential and popular ethnic festival. During the festival men and women would dress up in their traditional

的民族。泼水节是傣族最隆重的节日，也是云南少数民族节日中影响最大、参加人数最多的节日。每逢泼水节，傣族男女老少会穿上节日盛装，挑着清水，互相泼水，互祝吉祥、幸福、健康。人们一边翩翩起舞，一边泼水，象脚鼓声和铓锣之声响彻云霄，祝福的水花到处飞溅，场面十分壮观。

竹筒香茶是傣族人别具风味的一种茶饮，其制作方法甚为奇特，一般可分为五道程序：先将茶叶放

costumes, and carry buckets of clean water. Then they would splash water over each other and offer their heartfelt wishes and blessings to each other. People keep splashing while dancing to the resounding beat of elephant-foot drums and Mangluo gongs, making a spectacular scene.

The Dai Bamboo Canister-roast Tea is a very special tea variety found only among the Dai people. The processing of this tea is quite unusual, entailing the following five steps: load the tea leaves in a one-year-old fresh bamboo canister

• 西双版纳的傣族少女
Dai Girls in Xishuangbanna

在一个生长一年左右的嫩香竹竹筒中，分层装实；再将装有茶叶的竹筒放在火塘边烘烤，隔几分钟将竹筒翻动一次；待竹筒色泽由绿转黄时，筒内茶叶也已烤好；用刀劈开竹筒，取出清香扑鼻、形似长筒的竹筒香茶，将适量香茶置于碗中，用沸腾的开水冲泡，3—5分钟后即可饮用。这种竹筒茶喝起来既有茶的醇厚浓香，又有嫩竹的清香，别有一番醇美的茶味。

and press them layer by layer; place the canister by a fire and turn the canister every few minutes; when the canister turns from green to yellow, it indicates that the tea inside is well baked; remove the canister from the fire and hack it open, then one can find the cylinder-shaped tea emitting a delicate aroma; brew the tea in boiling water for 3–5 minutes before serving. As the drink blends both the aroma of the tea and the tender bamboo, this tea is amazingly refreshing.

• 傣族的竹筒香茶
The Dai Bamboo Canister-roast Tea

• 茶马古道上的傣族马帮
A Dai Caravan on the Ancient Tea-horse Road

傣家竹楼

  竹楼是傣族人世代居住的居所，属于干栏式建筑，造型美观。四方形的竹楼底层架空，没有墙壁，用来饲养牲畜和堆放杂物；楼上有堂屋和卧室，堂屋设火塘，是烧茶做饭和家人团聚的地方；外有开敞的前廊和晒台，前廊是白天工作、吃饭、休息和接待客人的地方，既明亮又通风；晒台是盥洗、晒衣、晾晒农作物和存放水罐的地方。这一廊一台是竹楼不可缺少的部分。这样的竹楼四面通风，可避虫兽侵袭，冬暖夏凉。而且当地每年雨量集中，洪水频发，竹楼楼下架空，墙又为多空隙的竹篾，很利于洪水的通过。傣族人喜欢在竹楼周围栽种凤尾竹、槟榔、芒果、香蕉等热带植物，使村寨充满诗情画意。

Dai's Bamboo Houses

For generations, the Dai people live in bamboo houses — beautiful stilted buildings. Beneath a platform, there is open space for keeping livestock and storage; on the upper level, the house is partitioned into bedrooms and a main living room with a fireplace, where the family cooks and gathers. There is also an open porch and a balcony, two indispensable elements in a bamboo house. The family works, dines, takes a break, and entertains guests on the porch; and does the laundry, dries clothes and crops, and stores pitchers on the balcony. Well-ventilated and comfortable, such a house makes a great residence. It can also keep pests and animals out. Furthermore, in the region where the Dai people live, heavy rainfall causes frequent floods during certain periods of a year. Such an stilted house with bamboo walls allows the water to pass through easily. The Dai people like to plant around their houses tropical plants such as fern leaf hedge bamboo, betel, mango, banana, etc., making the village full of poetic charm and picturesque beauty.

• 傣家竹楼
Dai's Bamboo Houses

基诺族与凉拌茶

　　基诺族主要分布在云南省西双版纳傣族自治州景洪市基诺乡，其余散居于基诺乡四邻山区。"基诺"意为"舅舅的后代"或"尊敬舅舅的民族"。据文献记载，因基诺山盛产普洱茶，明末清初有汉族商人进入，推广种茶、制茶技术，对基诺族社会的发展产生了积极影响。

　　在基诺族的传统观念里，茶与基诺族的发展进步密不可分，茶文化在基诺人生活的每一个角落。基诺族人每年都会进行祭祀茶神的活动，一般安排在春茶开采前，向茶神祈求茶叶丰收。吃过午饭就开始采茶了，人们会一边采茶一边唱起悠长的茶歌。

　　基诺族不仅喜欢煮饮茶汤，而且喜爱吃凉拌茶，这其实是中国古代食茶法的延续。制作方法是将刚采来的鲜嫩茶芽用手揉碎，放于碗内，再将新鲜的黄果叶揉碎，辣椒、大蒜切细，连同适量食盐投入盛有茶树嫩梢的碗中。最后，加上少许泉水，用筷子搅匀，放置一刻钟左右即可食用。凉拌茶不仅是

Jino People and Their Tea Salad

　　Most Jino people live in the Jino Village, Jinghong, Xishuangbanna Dai Autonomous Prefecture of the Yunnan Province. And one may also find some Jinos in the surrounding mountains. In their own language, "Jino" means "descendants of uncles" or the "people who respect their maternal uncles". According to historical records, during the late Ming and early Qing dynasties, some Han businessmen came to the Jino Mountain where natural Pu'er Tea grew. They taught the locals to cultivate and process the tea, having very positive impact on the development of Jino people's livelihood.

　　In Jino people's traditional conception, tea has an organic part of Jino people's life and has become an indispensable factor in the evolution and progress of the Jino civilization. Every year before the tea picking season in spring, Jino people would always hold rituals to worship the Tea God. They chanted prayers to the Tea God to pray for a bumper harvest. After lunch, people begin to pick tea leaves while singing long and sweet tea ballads.

　　In addition to drinking tea as a beverage, the Jino people also love

茶，也是一道菜，既可招待远方客人，又是基诺人日常吃米饭时的佐菜，它是基诺族茶文化中最具特色的一道风景。

● 基诺族少女
Jino Girls

to make salad with tea leaves. This is actually a tradition they inherited from ancient times. The recipe is as follows: rub and shred the tender tea buds and put them in a bowl; then shred fresh Huangguo leaves into small pieces; place the leaves into the bowl together with shredded pepper, garlic and some salt; add a little spring water and stir the mixture with chopsticks; let it sit for about a quarter of an hour before serving. More than a beverage, tea can also be a dish. Jino people use this tea salad to entertain guests from afar as well as a supplementary dish which goes well with rice in everyday meals. Indeed it is the most characteristic feature of the Jino tea culture.

● 正在晾晒烟丝的基诺族老人
An Old Jino Man Drying Cut Tobacco

哈尼族与土锅茶

哈尼族主要分布在云南西南部的西双版纳傣族自治州，以及新平、镇源、墨江、元江、红河等县。哈尼族村寨位置的选择颇为讲究，大都依山而建，背后是茂密的山林，山环水绕，梯田密布。哈尼族历史上传统民居有茅草房、蘑菇房、封火楼、土掌房、干栏房等多种形式。

Hani People and Their Native Pot Tea

The Hani people are mainly living in Xishuangbanna Dai Autonomous Prefecture of southwestern Yunnan, as well as in Xinping, Zhenyuan, Mojiang, Yuanjiang and Honghe counties. In general, Hani people are quite choosy about the location of their villages. Most villages are built by a river on the hillsides covered with dense forests. And around their villages,

- 哈尼族蘑菇房

蘑菇房是哈尼族传统建筑，形如蘑菇，多为土墙草顶，以木构架承重。房顶为四个斜坡面，上铺茅草，也有用瓦覆盖。房屋多分上中下三层，下层住牲畜，中层住人，上层堆放杂物。

Mushroom-shaped Cottages of the Hani people

The mushroom-shaped cottage, one of the traditional architectures of the Hani people, looks like a mushroom. It usually includes wood frame structure with clay walls and a thatch roof. Generally, the roof consists of four slope surfaces, covered with thatch sometimes with tiles. The cottage usually has three levels—the lower level is used as an enclosure for livestock, the middle level is for human dwelling, and the upper level is for storage.

哈尼族种植茶叶的历史相当久远，哈尼族地区的茶叶产量已占云南全省产量的三分之一。哈尼族的"土锅茶"是哈尼人待客的一种

Hani people cultivate many terraced lands. In villages, Hani people build a variety of houses, including thatched cottages, mushroom-shaped cottages, fire blocking

哈尼族新米节

新米节是哈尼族的传统节日，在每年农历七八月，当田里稻谷将熟的时候择日举行。节日这天早晨，每家户主来到稻田，选一个穗长粒大的稻穗，搓下少量稻谷，用树叶包好挂在田里，以示稻田多产稻谷。他们还会采一把谷穗带回家，舂出新米，做成新米饭，酿出新米酒，还要用新米爆出米花。晚饭之前，每家都要先用新米饭、新米爆的米花等作为供物来祭祀祖先，还要用米花喂狗。传说在古时候，一次大洪水把大地上所有的农作物都冲走了。水退后，一只小鸟发现了仅存的一穗稻谷，正要去啄食，一只小狗跳出来吓飞了小鸟，将谷种捡回给主人，从此人们才得以重新种植水稻。因此，每逢哈尼人吃新米，定要先给狗吃。祭祀活动结束，家人及宾客们才开始享用丰盛的谷饭、新米酒。据说，吃得越多越饱越好，秋收时稻谷才会粒粒饱满，永远吃不完。

Hani People's New Rice Festival

The New Rice Festival, one of the traditional festivals of Hani people, falls on an auspicious day between the 7th and 8th month of the Chinese lunar calendar when the paddy is about to ripe. On that day, heads of each family would go to their fields in the morning, pick a full-grown rice ear, rub off the grains, wrap them in a leaf and hang the package in the field as a sign of a bumper harvest. They also take home some paddy for rice and rice wine and rice pops. Before dinner, each family offers to their ancestors the newly-harvested rice and rice pops and they would also feed rice pops to dogs. As legend has it that once in ancient times, a horrible flood washed away all the crops growing on the land. After the flood, a bird found the only ear of rice left. When the bird was about to take it, a puppy jumped out of nowhere, scared away the bird and saved the last grain before brought it back to his master. With this grain, people were able to grow rice again. Hence, Hani people always feed their dogs first before enjoying the new rice. Having performed all the worship rituals, family members and guests would sit around the table to enjoy the sumptuous dinner of new rice and new rice wine. People also believe that the more one eats the more harvest one will get in the fall.

• 哈尼族姑娘
A Hani Girl

• 正在采茶的哈尼人
A Tea-picking Hani People

古老习俗。先用土陶锅把山泉水烧开，把烤制后的大叶茶放入锅内，煮10分钟左右，将茶水倒入竹制的茶杯中即可饮用。这种茶水汤色绿黄，品尝第一口时，会有一股极浓的青涩味，之后不久便觉得口中有回甘的茶香，令人回味无穷。

towers (*Fenghuo Lou*), clay houses and elevated houses.

Hani people have been engaging in tea production for many years. Tea produced in the areas inhabited by Hani people accounts for one third of the Yunnan's gross output. As a local tradition, Hani people would serve Pot Tea to guests as a way to express their hospitality. They first boil a pot of spring water; add roast large-leaf tea into the pot and boil it for about 10 minutes; serve the tea in bamboo cups. The tea water

拉祜族与糟茶

拉祜族源于甘肃、青海一带的古羌人，早期过着游牧生活，后来逐渐南迁，最终定居于澜沧江流域。现在的拉祜族主要分布在云南省澜沧江流域的普洱、临沧两地区，相邻的西双版纳及玉溪也有分布。在拉祜语中，"拉"意为老

- 拉祜族少女
  A Lahu Girl

looks greenish yellow and tastes bitter at the first sip, but soon a sweet aftertaste emerged and linger on.

Lahu People and Their Fermented Tea

As descendants of the ancient Qiang people lived in Gansu and Qinghai Provinces, Lahu people once led a nomadic life before moving southwards and settling down in the Lancang River basin. Nowadays, while most of the Lahu people live in Pu'er and Lincang of Yunnan Province, some are scattered in neighboring Xishuangbanna Dai Autonomous Prefecture and Yuxi. In their ethnic language, *La* means tiger and *Hu* means to roast meat. Hence hence the Lahu people are also known as tiger hunters.

According to research, Lahu people migrated to Xishuangbanna area during the early years of the Ming Dynasty (1368-1644). Influenced by the living style of the local people, Lahu people began to grow tea and gradually earned a living on tea cultivation. Today, these very old tea trees in Mount Mengsong and Mount Hekai in Menghai County of Xishuangbanna, are living witnesses of more than 500 years of tea-growing

拉祜族烤茶
Lahu People's Toast Tea

虎，"祜"意为将肉烤香，因此拉祜族被称为"猎虎的民族"。

据考证，明朝初年，拉祜族开始迁入云南西双版纳，受到当时西双版纳其他民族生产生活方式的影响，开始有规模地种植茶叶，并逐渐以茶为生。今天西双版纳傣族自治州勐海县勐宋和贺开两大古茶山中的古茶树，就是拉祜族500余年种茶历史的见证。

烤茶是拉祜族一种古老而普遍的饮茶方法：先将陶罐在火塘上烤热，然后放入茶叶进行炒制，待茶色焦黄时冲入开水，去掉浮沫后再加入开水。待茶煮好后，主人先倒少许茶水

history of Lahu people.

Roast Tea is an ancient but popular way of serving tea among Lahu people: preheat a pottery jar over a fire; add tea leaves to stir-fry; add boiling water when the tea turns brown; remove the foam and add more boiling water. Before serving the tea to guests, the host would sample the tea water to check the taste. If it is too strong, he will add boiling water to dilute it to the appropriate strength. With its rich aroma and strong taste, the tea is very refreshing.

Fermented Tea is another traditional way of serving tea among Lahu people. The ritual for this tea entails the following steps: first, boil fresh tea leaves in water

自尝，以试其浓度，如茶汁过浓，可加入开水使之浓淡相宜，然后再倒给客人饮用。这种烤茶香气很足，味道浓烈，饮后精神倍增。

糟茶也是拉祜族一种传统的饮茶方法。将鲜嫩茶叶采下后，加水在锅中煮至半熟，取出置于竹筒内存放发酵。饮用时，取少许放在开水中煮片刻，即可倒入茶盅饮用。这种茶略有苦涩酸味，饭后饮用有助消化，风味十分特别。

until they are half-cooked; second, take the tea leaves out and keep them in a bamboo canister for fermentation; third, take out a few leaves, and put them into boiling water for a short while before serving. The tea water has a very special, slightly bitter and sour taste which is good for digestion after meals

Lisu People and Their Thundering Tea

As a unique ethnic group with a long

- 傈僳族民间歌舞
A Folk Music and Dance Performance by Lisu people

傈僳族与雷响茶

傈僳族历史悠久，主要聚居于云南怒江傈僳族自治州。8世纪时，傈僳族先民居住在雅砻江、金沙江两岸的地区，15—19世纪，逐渐迁移到澜沧江和怒江流域。

傈僳族以服饰颜色分为白傈僳、黑傈僳、花傈僳。白傈僳、黑傈僳妇女服饰古朴，已婚妇女耳戴大铜环，头上以珍珠、贝壳、珊瑚为饰物，胸挂玛瑙、海贝或银币。花傈僳妇女服饰镶花边，头缠花布头巾，耳戴大铜环或银环，服饰色彩鲜艳。傈僳族男子喜欢青布包头，穿麻布长衫或短衫，左腰佩刀，右腰挂箭包。

喝雷响茶是傈僳人广为流传的一种古老的饮茶方法。先用一个大瓦罐将水煨开，再把茶饼放在小瓦罐里烤香，然后将大瓦罐里的开水加入小瓦罐熬茶；熬几分钟后，滤出茶叶渣，将茶汁倒入酥油筒内；倒入两三罐茶汁后加入酥油，再加事先炒熟、碾碎的核桃仁、花生米、盐巴或糖以及鸡蛋等；最后将一个在火中烧红的鹅卵石放入酥油筒内，使筒内茶汁"哧哧"作

history inhabited in Yunnan, the Lisu people concentrate mainly along the Nujiang River. Lisu people's ancestors once lived by the Yalong and Jinsha rivers during the 8th century before they migrated to the Lancang and Nujiang river basins between the 15th and 19th century.

By the color of their costumes, Lisu women can be further divided into subgroups of white, black and color. White and black Lisu women wear simple costumes. Married women wear large copper earrings, hair accessories made of pearls, shells or coral, and necklaces or brooches made of agate, seashells or silver coins. Color Lisu women wear lace dresses, colorful headpieces and large copper or silver earrings. Lisu men prefer blue turbans, linen gowns or shirts and wear their swords on the left side and arrow sacks on the right.

Serving Thundering Tea is an ancient but very popular practice among Lisu people. The process entails the following: simmer a large crock of water; roast a cake-shaped compressed tea in a small crock until it emits the aroma; add the boiling water to the smaller crock and boil the tea for a few minutes; sift the tea dross, and pour two or three crocks of the tea water into a container and add butter, fried and

响，犹如雷响一般；响声过后马上使劲用木杵上下抽打，使酥油成为雾状，均匀溶于茶汁中；打好后倒出，趁热饮用。经过打制的茶汁香味和浓度都得以提高，风味独特。

crushed walnuts, peanuts, salt or sugar, and eggs; then put into a red-hot pebble, which makes the liquid sizzle like thundering; immediately after the sound dies away, stir the mixture to dissolve the butter in the tea; finally serve the tea and drink it while it's hot. Extra ingredients increase the flavor of the tea. It is indeed a unique experience.

- 云南香格里拉最大的傈僳族村寨——同乐村
  Tongle Village—the Largest Lisu Community in Shangri-La, Yunnan Province

傈僳族的刀杆节

　　刀杆节又名"爬刀节",是傈僳族一年一度的传统节日,时间是在每年农历二月初八。"上刀山,下火海"是刀杆节中主要的表演活动,它再现了山地民族翻山越岭的生活经历。刀杆节这天,几名健壮的傈僳族男子先表演"下火海"。他们赤裸双脚,在烧红的火炭堆里跳跃翻滚,用火炭抹脸,并且互相传递烧得通红的火链,直到把炭火全部踏灭下火海活动才结束。第二天,他们把磨快的36把长刀,刀口向上分别用藤条横绑在两根20多米高的木杆上,做成一个刀梯。表演者空手赤足,踩着快刀的刃口攀上木杆顶端,并在杆顶表演各种高难度动作,颂祝人畜平安、五谷丰登。下面观看的人们点燃鞭炮,鞭炮声、鼓声、歌舞声和欢呼声齐发,大家载歌载舞,场面热闹非凡。

• 傈僳族刀杆节上"上刀山"表演（图片提供：FOTOE）
A Show of "Climbing a Mountain of Blades" at Lisu People's Blades-pole Festival

Lisu People's Blades-pole Festival

The Blades-pole Festival (also known as the Blades Climbing Festival), a traditional annual event of Lisu people, falls on the 8th day of the second month of the Chinese lunar calendar. During the festival, men would perform the traditional show "climbing the blades pole and passing through the ames", which reproduces the arduous early life of their ancestors. On the first day of the festival, several robust Lisu men would perform the Passing through the Flames ritual: they jump onto a heap of red-hot charcoals on barefoot, smudge their faces with charcoal, and pass around burning-hot iron chains. The show will not be over until they put off the charcoal flame completely through their dancing. On the following day, they set up a ladder with two twenty meters high parallel poles and fasten thirty-six sharpened long knives horizontally with blades facing upwards to form the rungs. The performers would climb up to the top of the blade ladder on bare feet and bare hands. They would also perform on the top of the poles all kinds of difficult movements, and express their best wishes and blessings for the people and their livestock. People watching the show would set off firecrackers, sing and dance around. The festival reaches its climax in the orchestra of firecrackers, drums, singing and dancing, cheering and laughing.

白族与三道茶

在中国云南西部以洱海为中心的大理，生活着勤劳善良的白族人。白族历史悠久，由于风俗尚白，历史上曾有"白人"之称。白族在天文、历法、医学、文学等领域都取得过灿烂的成就。白族有自己的语言，但大多数白族群众都通晓汉语，并把汉语作为与其他民族交流的工具。著名的大理崇圣寺三塔、剑川石钟山石窟造像等，都显

Bai People and Their Three-course Tea

The industrious and kind-hearted Bai people live mostly in Dali Bai Autonomous Prefecture which centers around the Erhai Lake, in western Yunnan Province. With a long history and a preference for white color, Bai people were also known as the "white people". Bai people made outstanding achievements in many fields such as astronomy, calendar, medicine and

示了白族人在建筑、雕刻、绘画等方面的卓越才能。

　　白族人在逢年过节、生辰寿诞、男婚女嫁、拜师学艺等喜庆日子里，或是在亲朋宾客来访之际，都会以特有的"三道茶"待客。第一道茶，称为"清苦之茶"，寓意为人立业要先吃苦。制作时，先将水烧开，再由司茶者将一只小砂罐置于文火上烘烤，待罐烤热后，随即取适量茶叶放入罐内，并不停地转动砂罐，使茶叶均匀受热。待罐

literature. Although Bai people have their own ethnic language, most of them understand Mandarin and use it as a means of communication with other people. Bai people are also very skillful in architecture, sculpture and painting. The famous Three Pagodas at the Chongsheng Temple in Dali and the statues in the grottos of Shizhong Mountain in Jianchuan fully demonstrate their skills in these regards.

During festivals and special occasions such as birthday parties, weddings, and apprenticeship initiation ceremonies, or when entertaining

- **正在制作扎染布的白族女子**

扎染是白族人的传统民间工艺，原料为棉麻质地的白布，染料为苍山上生长的蓼蓝、板蓝根、艾蒿等天然植物的蓝靛溶液。制作时，根据花样纹式用线将白布缚着，做成一定襞褶的小纹，浸入染缸里浸染。如此反复浸染到一定程度后，取出晾干，拆去缬结，便出现蓝底白花的图案花纹来。这些图案多由简单的几何图形组成，构图严谨，布局丰满，充满生活气息。

A Bai Women Working on Tie-dye

Tie-dye is a traditional art and craft of Bai people. They dye white cotton or linen cloth with indigo pigments made of natural indigo knotweed, roots of Isatis indigotica, moxa, etc. The production process of tie-dye entails the following: first fold the cloth into a certain pattern, tie it with strings, and dip it into a vat of dye water several times before drying and removing the string knots. Tie-dyed cloth presents white patterns on a blue background. By careful combination and arrangement of simple geometric graphics, the patterns are full of vigor and vitality.

- **剑川石钟山石窟造像**

  石钟山石窟位于云南省大理白族自治州剑川县城西南30千米的石宝山南部，开凿于南诏、大理时期，共有17窟139躯造像，包括本主、佛、菩萨、明王、天王、头陀僧等，具有浓厚的佛教密宗色彩，它依山而凿，宏伟壮观，是云南境内现存规模最大、保存完好的佛教石窟群，也是古代白族人民的石窟艺术杰作。

The Grottos on the Stone Clock Mountain at Jianchuan County

Grottos on the Stone Clock Mountain are hidden in the southern face of Mount Shibao, some 30 kilometers southwest of the county seat Jianchuan, Dali Bai Autonomous Prefecture. The grottos and the sculptures were believed to be built during the periods of Nanzhao and Dali kingdoms. There remains 139 statues in 17 grottos, depicting the Patron, Buddha, Bodhisattva, deities and reverent monks of Esoteric Buddhism. These magnificent grottos are the largest and best-preserved existing Buddhist grottos in Yunnan Province as well as grotto art masterpieces of the ancient Bai people.

内茶叶"啪啪"作响，叶色转黄，发出焦糖香时，立即注入已经烧沸的开水。少顷，司茶者将沸腾的茶水倾入茶盅，再用双手举盅献给客人。由于这种茶经烘烤、煮沸而成，因此，看上去色如琥珀，闻起

friends and relatives, Bai host usually offers the guest a three-course tea. The first course is known as the Bitter Tea, metaphorically symbolizing that all success has been built on hardworking and suffering. A tea master first preheats a pot on slow fire before adding tea leaves

来焦香扑鼻，喝下去滋味苦涩。

　　第二道茶称为"甜茶"。客人喝完第一道茶后，司茶者重新用小砂罐置茶、烤茶、煮茶，同时要在茶盅中放入少许红糖，再将煮好的茶汤倾入盅内，约八分满。这道茶甜中带香，寓意苦尽甘来。

to the pot for baking; while baking, he turns the pot constantly to enable even heating of the tea leaves; when the leaves turn yellow and emit a slightly burned but sweet aroma and make a "papa" sound, add boiling water to the pot, and brew the tea water a short while before serving it hot in a cup. Usually, the person serving

- **大理白族三月街的舞龙活动**

  三月街是大理白族人的传统节日和贸易集市，每年农历三月十五日至二十一日在大理古城西举行。在此期间，人们从四面八方赶来参加交易，热闹非凡，交易物资以骡马、山货、药材、茶叶为主。三月街上，白族人还会举行对歌、跳舞、赛马等活动。

  Loong Dance at Bai People's March Fair, Dali Bai Autonomous Prefecture

  The March Fair, a traditional festival as well as a market fair of Bai people living around Dali, opens on the 15th day and ends on the 21st day of the third month of the Chinese lunar calendar. On this occasion, people coming around gather in the west part of the Old Town of Dali and deal in mules, horses, mountain products, medicinal herbs and tea. Bai people also engage themselves in duet singing, dancing, horse racing and other entertaining activities.

● 白族的三道茶 (图片提供: FOTOE)
Bai People's Three-course Tea

tea would hold the cup with both hands and present it to the guest. The baked-tea water looks brownish like amber, has a slightly burnt but very agreeable smell, and tastes bitter and raw.

Sweet Tea, the second course tea is served after the guest finishes the bitter tea. The host serving the tea repeats the same procedures of baking the tea leaves in the small pot and brewing it on fire. Different from the first course, he puts some brown sugar in the cup before pouring the brewed tea into the cup to 80% full. This tea is delightfully sweet, implying that hard work will be repaid.

Aftertaste Tea, the third course tea is served last. Preparation of the third course tea follows the same procedures as the two previous courses. Instead of brown sugar, some honey, pop-rice, pepper, and walnuts are added to the infusion. In general, guests are advised to take the tea while shaking the cup to enable better mixture of the ingredients. This tea is of mixed-flavors: sweet, sour, bitter and spicy, and leaves plenty of aftertastes.

第三道茶称为"回味茶"。其煮茶方法与前面基本相同，只是茶盅中放的原料已换成适量蜂蜜、少许炒米花、若干粒花椒，以及一撮核桃仁。饮第三道茶时一般是一边晃动茶盅，使茶汤和作料均匀混合，一边趁热饮下。这杯茶喝起来甜、酸、苦、辣，各味俱全，回味无穷。

纳西族与"龙虎斗"

纳西族是以中国云南为主要聚居地的少数民族，主要居住在云南西北的丽江、宁蒗、维西、香格里拉、德钦等地，四川的盐源、木里等地也有分布。纳西族历史悠久，与中国古代氐、羌等游牧民族有渊源关系，史称"牦牛夷"。纳西族有自己的语言，用象形文字书写的《东巴经》，是世界闻名的古文字资料，香格里拉市三坝乡白地则是东巴文化的发源地。

纳西族人性格开朗，能歌善舞，每逢喜庆节日，就燃起熊熊篝火，举行跳舞等活动。纳西族的文化艺术丰富多彩，而纳西族聚居的

Naxi People and Their "Loong Tiger Fight"

Naxi people is a unique ethnic group inhabited mostly in the northwestern part of Yunnan Province (Lijiang, Ninglang, Weixi Lisu Autonomous County, Shangri-La City, and Deqin County). Some settled in Yanyuan and Muli counties of Sichuan Province. Historically known as people of the yaks, Naxi people have a long history and their ancestors may be traced back to ancient Di, Qiang and other nomads. Naxi people have their own language and pictographic characters. The *Dongba Scripture* is a world-famous literature written in this ancient script. It is commonly believed that Baidi at the Sanba Village, Shangri-La is the birthplace of the Dongba culture.

Outgoing and talented, Naxi people love to sing and dance around bonfires during festivals or happy occasions. They also enjoy colorful art and culture. In the Old Town of Lijiang inhabited by Naxi

• 纳西族少女
Naxi Girls

丽江古城，其建筑具有独特的民族风格和珍贵的艺术价值。

纳西族有一种特殊的茶俗，称为"龙虎斗"，纳西语叫"阿吉勒烤"，其饮用方法非常有趣。将茶放在小陶罐中烘烤，待茶焦黄后，冲入开水，像熬中药一样，熬得浓浓的。同时，将半杯白酒倒入茶盅，再将熬好的茶汁冲进酒里，这时茶盅发出"啪啪"的响声，响声

people, local architecture incorporates many distinctive ethnic elements as well as ingredients of high artistic value.

Naxi people have a special way of serving tea known as the "Loong Tiger Fight". Preparation of this tea is quite interesting: first bake the tea leaves in a small pot until they turn brown; add boiling water to the pot; brew the tea until the infusion becomes thick like decoction of herbal medicine; fill up the tea cup

- 丽江纳西族民居
Traditional Naxi Houses at Lijiang City

过后，就可以饮用了。有人还会加点辣椒。据当地人说，感冒的人喝一杯龙虎斗，周身出汗，睡一觉后就感到头不昏，浑身有力，感冒也好了大半。

with liquor to half-full, and then add tea. Serve the tea after the sputtering sound dies away. Sometimes, chili pepper is also added. The locals say that this punch could relieve cold symptoms.

- **"高原明珠"泸沽湖**

泸沽湖位于四川省凉山彝族自治州与云南省丽江市之间，四周林木葱郁，空气清新，湖水清澈如镜，景色迷人，被誉为"高原明珠"。湖边居住的摩梭人还将泸沽湖奉为"母亲湖"。

Lugu Lake— "Pearl on the Plateau"

Surrounded by forests, the Lugu Lake lies between Liangshan Yi Autonomous Prefecture of Sichuan Province and Lijiang City of Yunnan Province and is known as the Pearl on the Plateau for the fresh air, clear water and spectacular scenery. The Mosuo people, native inhabitants living around the lake, worship the lake as their Mother Lake.

纳西族的东巴文化

千百年来，纳西族信奉"东巴教"，由此孕育了丰富博大的东巴文化。东巴教的祭司称为"东巴"，意为"智者"，是纳西族最高级的知识分子，东巴文化的主要传承者。而东巴文化包括象形文字、东巴经、东巴绘画、东巴音乐舞蹈等。其中，东巴文字是世界上仅存的还在使用的象形文字，被誉为"东巴文化的瑰宝"。它是纳西族在东巴教的经书中使用的一种图画文字，由东巴用竹尖笔或铜尖笔蘸上用松明烟和酒、胶水、胆汁调制成的墨汁，写在树皮制的厚纸上。用东巴文写成的《东巴经》，堪称丰富的纳西族百科全书，记录了纳西族的神话、叙事诗、民谣、谚语等，为研究纳西族历史、宗教、生活习俗等提供了宝贵的资料。

- **纳西族东巴文古籍**

东巴文创始于唐代，是一种兼备表意和表音成分的图画象形文字。东巴文有1400多个单字，词语丰富，能表达细腻的情感，能记录复杂的事件，亦能写诗作文，在世界文字发展史上堪称奇迹。

Ancient Literature Written in Dongba Hieroglyph

Created during the Tang Dynasty, the Dongba written language is a hieroglyph with both the ideographic and phonetic elements. With more than 1,400 individual words, the Dongba hieroglyph is arranged in a great number of combinations to express delicate feelings, describe complicated events, and even compose proses and poems. Indeed, the Domba hieroglyph is like a godsend in the evolution of written languages.

Naxi People's Dongba Culture

For over one thousand years, Naxi peplple believe in Dongba religion, and built a rich culture. Referred to as the Dongba (which means a wise man), the priest is the savant among Naxi people and the main promoter of the native culture which includes, among others, Dongba hieroglyph, Dongba scripture, paintings, music and dance. Dongba symbols, the only hieroglyph still in use in the world, is regarded as the Gem of the Dongba Culture. Dongbas (priests) use bamboo or copper stylus and ink made of alcohol, glue, gall and the black fume off a burning resin-covered pinewood, to draw the hieroglyph on thick bark-made paper. The *Dongba Scripture* is an encyclopedia about Naxi people and their culture. It covers a wide range of subjects in different genres such as native myths, epics, ballads and proverbs. It offers an invaluable source of information for studies of the history, religion, customs and other aspects of the Naxi civilization.

- 跳东巴舞的纳西族老东巴

作为东巴教的祭司，东巴在纳西族中地位很高，被视为人与神鬼之间的媒介，既能与神打交道，又能与鬼说话，能迎福驱鬼，消除民间灾难，给人间带来安乐。

An Old Dongba Performing a Sacred Dongba Dance

As priests of the Dongba religion, Dongbas are highly respected by Naxi people. They are believed to be the media between the living and the deities. They give blessings and practice exorcism to help eliminate suffering and bring peace and happiness to the world.

彝族与烤茶

彝族是中国古老的民族之一，主要分布在云南、四川、贵州三省和广西壮族自治区的西北部。彝族先民早在远古时期就开始在滇池、邛都（现四川西昌东南）等地生息繁衍。

火把节是彝族最盛大的传统节日，在每年的农历六月二十四日。传说古时彝族百姓为了反抗一个暴

- 云南彝族少女

Yi People and Their Roast Tea

Yi people, one of the ancient ethnic groups of the Chinese nation, live mostly in Yunnan, Sichuan, Guizhou Provinces and the northwestern part of Guangxi Zhuang Autonomous Region. As early as in ancient times, Yi people's ancestors settled down in Dianchi Lake, Qiongdu (present day southeast of Xichang County, Sichuan Province) areas where they lived and bred until this day.

The Torch Festival, the grandest traditional festival of Yi people, falls on the 24th day of the sixth month of the

A Yi Teenage Girl

● 云南新平的彝族村寨
A Yi Village at Xinping Yi and Dai Autonomous County, Yunnan Province

虐的土司而起义，为了庆祝胜利，人们便把胜利的那一天定为火把节。对彝族同胞来说，火把节如同汉族的春节一样，特别隆重。点火把是火把节里最隆重的一项活动。节日到来之前，人们从山上砍回箭竹或割回蒿草，晒干扎成火把。过节时人们点燃篝火，载歌载舞，彻夜狂欢。火把节一般欢庆三天，头一天全家欢聚，后两天举办摔跤、赛马、斗牛、竞舟、拔河等丰富多彩的活动。

作为最早发现、制作和饮用

Chinese lunar calendar. As legend has it, this festival was observed by Yi people to celebrate the victory of an uprising against a tyrannical chieftain in ancient times. The festival is celebrated in such grandeur which is comparable to the Spring Festival of Han People. During the Torch Festival, torch ignition is the most important activity. Before the festival, people would collect sword bamboo (*Fargesia*) or wormwood and dry them to make torches. During the festival, people would light up bonfire and torches, sing and dance through the night. Generally,

茶的民族之一，彝族总是将茶放在酒和肉之前的位置，至今在西南彝族聚居区，烤茶及"一茶二酒三食肉"的习俗仍然到处可见。彝族烤茶的方法颇为讲究，先将绿茶放入烤热的铜制或陶制茶罐内焙烤，直至茶叶酥脆、略黄时，灌入事先加热的水少许，待罐内茶水泡沫稍息，再冲入热水至满，又于火上煨

this festival lasts for three days: the first day featured family reunion, and the following two days featured a variety of activities including, among others, wrestling, horse racing, bull-fighting, boat racing, and tug-of-war contests.

As one of the ethnic groups who discovered, processed and consumed tea first, Yi people always place tea before wine and meat. Even today, in the areas in habited by Yi people in southwestern China, Roast Tea and a custom to place tea before wine and meat are still popular. the areas inhabited by Yi people are very particular about their Roast Tea: they first bake the green tea in a preheated copper or clay teapot till the tea becomes crispy and slightly yellow; add a little hot water to the pot and wait for the bubbles to disappear; and add more hot water to fill the pot; brew the tea over slow fire for a while and remove the pot from the heater; let the tea sit for a while and filter the tea water into a cup; add salt, fried

• 四川凉山彝族男子服饰
Men's Costume of Yi People at Liangshan Yi Autonomous Prefecture, Sichuan Province

● 火把节上的彝族虎舞
The Yi's Tiger Dance at the Torch Festival

煮片刻便可起罐，让茶叶沉淀一会儿，方倒出茶水过滤，内加盐、炒米、核桃粉、芝麻等即可饮用。彝族的烤茶色、香、味俱佳。

藏族与酥油茶

藏族是中国西部的少数民族，主要分布在西藏，其余分布在四川、青海、甘肃、云南等地。藏族人大多信奉具有浓厚地方色彩的藏传佛教，把活佛高僧尊为上人，藏语称为"喇嘛"，故藏传佛教又被称为"喇嘛教"。由于藏族人大多

rice, crushed walnut, sesame seeds before serving. The tea features outstanding appearance, aroma and texture.

Zang People and the Butter Tea

With a population of about 7 million, Zang people inhabit mostly in Xizang, with some scattered in other provinces including Sichuan, Qinghai, Gansu and Yunnan. Most Zang people believe in native Zang Buddhism and respect the living Buddhas and high-ranking monks as exalted personages, Lama in the Zang language. Therefore, Zang Buddhism is also known as Lamaism. As Zang people

生活在世界屋脊——青藏高原上，衣食住行、婚丧嫁娶、礼俗节日都带有鲜明的高原印记。糌粑、酥油茶和青稞酒是藏族人的生活必需品。

酥油茶是一种在茶汤中加入酥油等原料，再经特殊方法加工而成的茶。所谓酥油，就是把牛奶或羊奶煮沸，用勺搅拌，倒入竹桶内，冷却后凝结在溶液表面的一层脂肪。至于茶叶，一般选用的是紧压茶类中的普洱茶、金尖等。酥油

live on the roof of the world — the Qinghai-Xizang Plateau, the Plateau has a direct impact on every aspect of their life, including basic necessities, wedding and funeral customs, rites and festivals. Tsam-pa (baked barley cake), butter tea and barley wine are part of their diet.

Butter Tea is a tea beverage made of tea and butter after a special preparation process. Zang people use yak or goat milk to make butter: boil, stir and pour the milk into a bamboo bucket; and collect the butter (the surface layer of fat) after the milk cools and congeals. To make the Butter Tea, they usually use compressed tea varieties such as Pu'er or Jinjian (Golden Tip) as the main ingredient and follow a particular preparation process: first boil a pot of water, crush the compressed tea with a knife and add it to the pot and brew it in boiling water for about half an hour; then filter out the tea dross and fill a cylindrical tea-maker with the tea water,

- 身着节日盛装的藏族姑娘
  Zang Girls in Their Festival Attire

- **茶马古道旁的碉房**

碉房是青藏高原上常见的藏族民居建筑形式，一般为石头砌成，墙壁大都上薄下厚，最厚处可达1米，整面墙呈梯形，平顶。碉房多为多层建筑，底层可以蓄养牲畜，二层可以作人的居室、储藏室等，三层可以作经堂，供佛像、点酥油灯等。

Tower-houses Standing by the Ancient Tea-horse Road

Tower-houses, the most common Zang residence on the Qinghai-Xizang Plateau, are built generally with stone walls: thick walls up to one meter thick on the lower levels and thinner upper part. Therefore the walls take trapezoid form. Most tower-houses have flat roofs and several storeys. People use the ground level as enclosures holding the livestock, the second level for bedrooms and storage space, and the third level for prayer rooms where the statutes of Buddha are worshipped and oil lamps are lit.

茶的加工方法比较讲究，一般先用一口锅烧水，待水煮沸后，再用刀子把紧压茶切碎，放入沸水中煮半小时左右，待茶汁浸出后，滤去茶叶，把茶汁装进长圆柱形的打茶桶内。与此同时，用另一口锅煮牛奶，一直煮到表面凝结一层酥油时，把它倒入盛有茶汤的打茶筒内，再放上适量的酥油、盐和糖。这时，盖住打茶筒，用手握住直立茶筒之中能上下移动的长棒，不断舂打。根据藏族人的经验，直到筒

boil a pot of milk while tea is being brewed till the cream layer accumulates on the top; pour the milk into the tea-maker and add some butter, salt and sugar; put the lid on and put a the stick vertically into the tea-maker and stir the mixture. According to Zang people's experience, the tea is ready to serve when the sound changes from Bang-bang-bang to Chow-chow-chow, indicating that the tea is blended with butter, salt and sugar. The Butter Tea offers mixed flavors in an agreeable combination. The Qinghai-Xizang Plateau is sparsely

内声音由"咣当咣当"变成"嚓咿嚓咿"时，茶、奶、酥油、盐、糖等即已混为一体，酥油茶就打好了。酥油茶滋味多样，喝起来涩中带甘，咸里透香。在青藏高原地带，人烟稀少，家中很少有客登门。偶尔有客临门，可以招待的东西不多，加上酥油茶本身具有的独特作用，自然成了款待宾客的珍贵之物了。

populated and people live far away from each other. Visitors are not so common due to severe geological and climatic conditions. When guests do visit, there is little refreshment to entertain them. Naturally, the Butter Tea, in addition to being a special beverage for everyday consumption, becomes one of the choice food for the hosts to show their hospitality to the guests.

- **酥油茶的制作**

打酥油茶用的茶筒多为铜质或银质。而盛酥油茶用的茶具多为银质，甚至还有用黄金加工而成的。茶碗虽以木碗为多，但常常是用金、银或铜镶嵌而成。更有甚者，有用翡翠制成的，这些华丽而又昂贵的茶具，常被看作传家之宝。而这些不同等级的茶具，又是人们财产拥有程度的标志。

Making the Butter Tea

Usually, Zang people use bronze or silver tea-makers, silver or even gold teapots, and wooden cups often inlaid with gold, silver or copper. Some tea cups are even made of jade. Such dazzling, expensive tea sets are often viewed as family heirlooms. All those tea sets of different materials may also reflect the wealth the owners have.

康巴汉子

传统上的藏族聚居区按方言可以划分成卫藏、康巴、安多三部分。以拉萨为中心向西辐射的高原大部称为"卫藏",是藏区政治、宗教、文化中心;念青唐古拉山—横断山以北的藏北、青海、甘南、川西北大草原称为"安多";川西的甘孜、阿坝,西藏的昌都和云南的迪庆称为"康巴"。

Men of Kamba

Traditionally, the areas inhabited by Zang people can be divided by dialects into three parts: Weizang, Kamba and Amdo. Weizang includes Lhasa and its peripheral areas in the west covering most part of the Plateau. It is the political, religious and cultural center of the areas inhabited by Zang people. Amdo refers to the great grassland lying in the north of Nyenchen Tanglha (or Nyainqêntanglha) Mountains — Hengduan Mountains, including northern Xizang, Qinghai, southern Gansu, and northwestern Sichuan. Kamba includes Ganzi and Aba Zang Autonomous Prefectures in western Sichuan, Qamdo of Xizang and Diqing of Yunnan.

• 康巴藏族男子
A Man of the Kamba Region

古道驿镇

Towns on the Ancient Tea-horse Road

　　茶马古道的兴旺和延伸，推动了高原驿镇的发展。许多商队和马帮集中驻足停留、进行商品交易的驿站，往往后来就成了繁荣的城镇。

The prosperity and extension of the Ancient Tea-horse Road promoted the development of plateau posts where caravans and horse troops stopped over to do business. Many eventually grew into flourishing towns.

> 茶叶发源之地西双版纳

西双版纳傣族自治州位于云南省西南端，与老挝、缅甸山水相连，与泰国、越南为近邻。西双版纳，古代傣语为"勐巴拉那西"，

西双版纳的茶园
A Tea Plantation in Xishuangbanna Dai Autonomous Prefecture

> Xishuangbanna: Place of Origin of Tea

Xishuangbanna Dai Autonomous Prefecture in the southwestern corner of Yunnan Province, shares border with Laos and Myanmar and neighbors with Thailand and Vietnam. In the ancient Dai language, Xishuangbanna means "ideal and amazing paradise". Just as it implies, Xishuangbanna is widely known for its spectacular tropical rainforests and hospitality of the native people. The warm and humid climate offers excellent condition for the growth of luxuriant forests and vegetation. The land is hence also known as the "Kingdom of Flora".

Xishuangbanna is one of the places where tea was first discovered and cultivated in China, with local Pu'er Tea as the oldest and most iconic symbol of such civilization. There are several

西双版纳的南传佛教寺庙
A Theravada Buddhist Temple in Xishuangbanna Dai Autonomous Prefecture

意思是"理想而神奇的乐土",以神奇的热带雨林自然景观和少数民族风情闻名于世。这里终年温暖,树木四季常青,而且常年湿润多雨,森林繁茂,植物繁多,被誉为"植物王国"。

西双版纳是中国最古老的茶叶发源地之一,而普洱茶是西双版纳历史最悠久、最有标志性的文明符号。西双版纳境内现有13万亩保存较为完好的古茶园,是研究茶叶历史的珍贵资源,又是生产高档普洱

well-preserved ancient tea plantations (about 8667 hectares) where some very old tea trees still grow, allowing for tea-related historical studies as well as offering fine Pu'er Tea for high-end market consumption. As early as in the Tang Dynasty, local tea was already sold to Xizang and other regions. During the Song Dynasty, in addition to trading with Yunnan-Xizang area in tea and horses, the Dali Kingdom also sent envoys to Guangxi, Jiangnan (a region south of the Yangtze River, including some parts of Jiangsu and Anhui and northern areas of

茶的优质资源。西双版纳所产的茶叶早在唐代就销往西藏等地，宋朝除与滇藏地区进行茶马交易外，大理国还派使臣到广西、江南，甚至中原一带用普洱茶做茶马交易。明朝至清朝中期，西双版纳普洱茶的生产达到鼎盛时期，澜沧江两岸的各大古茶山，年产干茶十万余担。运茶古道上商旅塞途，构成了一幅边塞风情与茶马古道交相辉映的历史画卷。

Zhejiang), and even the Central Plains to conduct the tea-horse mutual trade. Between the Ming and the mid-Qing dynasties, local Pu'er Tea production reached a record high with the gross output of major tea plantations along the Lancang River reaching more than 5 million kilograms per year. The Ancient Tea-horse Road crowded with caravans, became an integral part of charming borderland history.

Within Xishuangbanna, the road through pristine forests was a 100-kilometer-long, 1-to-1.5-meter-

- 西双版纳傣族泼水节

Dai People Celebrating Their Water-splashinp Festival (Songkran)

西双版纳境内的茶马古道约100千米，大部分位于原始密林中，古道宽1—1.5米，由当时官府和当地茶庄共同投资修建，采用山中的青石砌成路面，危险路段用条石筑基，还建有防止土石坍塌的石壁。

wide trail. With joint investment of the then government and local tea plantation owners, the road was paved with stone slates. In sections where the terrains were dangerous and unsafe, stone foundations were built to support the road. Stone walls were also built to prevent landslides.

勐海南糯山

南糯山在西双版纳州勐海县东部，是西双版纳有名的茶叶产地，漫山遍野都是茶园。南糯山最早什么时候开始种茶已不可考，但可以肯定的是，南诏时期布朗族的先民还在此种茶，后来布朗族迁离南糯山，遗留的茶山被哈尼族的一支——僾尼人继承，僾尼人已经在南糯山生活了57—58代，已经历1100多年的时间。这里生长着一株树龄超过800年的栽培型茶树王，现在仍四季郁郁葱葱，南糯山因此被誉为"茶树王之乡"。由于当地茶叶的品质优良，过去大批马帮会在每年农历十月进入村庄，将茶叶运到普洱、勐海、勐腊等地贩卖，还有些大型马帮直接就将茶叶贩至东南亚的许多国家。

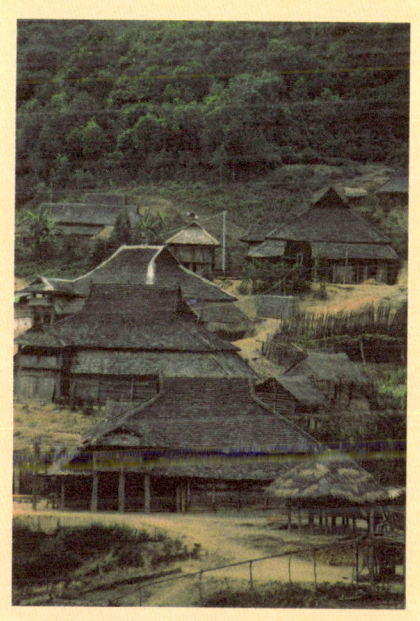

• 南糯山僾尼人的房屋
Houses of the Aini People at Mount Nannuo

Mount Nannuo, Menghai

Situated in the eastern part of Menghai County, Xishuangbanna Dai Autonomous Prefecture, Mount Nannuo is a well-known tea growing area where tea plantations cluster. There is no documented evidence about the exact time when people started to grow tea here. But historical records show that the ancestors of Blang people were already growing tea there during the Nanzhao Kingdom Period (738-937); later when Blang people moved, Aini people — a branch of Hani ethnic group inherited the tea plantations and lived there for 57 or 58 generations over a period of more than 1,100 years. There remains an 800-year-old tea tree which is green all year long and known as the Tea Tree King. Mount Nannuo is hence also known as the "hometown of the Tea Tree King". Local tea enjoyed a reputation for its fine quality. As a result, every 10th month of the Chinese lunar calendar, caravans would flood into Nannuo Mountain and ship the tea to other places such as Pu'er City and Menghai and Mengla counties for sale. Some large caravans even shipped the tea to many Southeast Asian countries directly.

贡茶产地易武

易武古镇在西双版纳州勐腊县西北。这里山高雾重，土地肥沃，湿热多雨，是种植茶叶的理想之地。易武的兴盛起始于明代，不仅因为它是古六大茶山之一，更重要的是这里曾经是一个集产茶、制茶、易茶为一体的热闹繁华的茶叶集散地。历史上，由于康藏地区对茶的大量需求，产自六大茶山的普洱茶就源源不断地由骡马队从易武运出，经普洱，到下关，过丽江，进四川，最后来到康藏地区，甚至到达世界屋脊的中印、中尼、中锡边境。

为了便于骡队马帮的运输，清道光年间铺设了从思茅关至倚邦、易武长达240千米、宽约1.6米，被称为"五尺道"的青石路，它连通了六大茶山。石板路修通后，许多茶商马队纷纷前来易武，马道上终年驮铃回荡，造就了易武

• 易武正山茶饼
"Zhengshan" Compressed Tea Cakes Made in Yiwu Town

历史上茶庄林立、商贾云集的兴盛景象。在易武繁盛时期，除了滇藏之间的这条开辟最早、持续时间最长的茶马古道外，茶商还开辟了一条从易武到老挝，转越南，走南洋的"茶马道"。清代末年，随着茶叶贸易的式微，易武的茶马古道逐渐被乱草所湮没，只有古道上光滑的青石板记录了当年的辉煌。

由于易武镇气候温暖湿润、雨量充沛，周围茶园密布，至今仍然保持种茶、采茶、制茶的传统。其中，著名的七子饼茶和元宝茶是易武镇的特产。元宝茶在清代曾是进贡宫廷的贡茶，并行销到全国各地和东南亚地区。当地至今还保留着当年进贡茶叶的茶树。

- 易武古镇的茶马古道
A Section of the Ancient Tea-horse Road in the Ancient Town of Yiwu

Yiwu: Place of Origin of Tribute Tea

Situated in the northwest of Mengla County, Xishuangbanna Dai Autonomous Prefecture, the ancient town of Yiwu is one of the ideal places to grow tea for its high elevation, heavy fog, fertile soil, warm temperature and high humidity. The town started to expand in the Ming Dynasty, not only because it hosted one of the six famous tea growing mountains but also because it was a busy distribution center where people grew, processed and traded tea. Historically, driven by the large demand for tea in the areas inhabited by Zang people, shipment of Pu'er Tea from the six tea-growing mountains never ceased. Caravans picked up tea at Yiwu, carried it all the way through Pu'er, Xiaguan and Lijiang to Sichuan Province, and arrived at the destinations in the areas inhabited by Zang people, some even further to the border areas between China and India, Nepal and Ceylon.

To facilitate the caravans, a slate trail between Fort Simao and Yiwu (Yibang) was paved during the reign of Emperor Daoguang of the Qing Dynasty. This 240-kilometer-long and 1.6-meter-wide trail, known as the "Five-*Chi*-road" (*Chi*, a Chinese unit of length, 1 *Chi* ≈ 0.33

meter), linked up all the six tea-growing mountains. After its completion, the trail brought more caravans to Yiwu, helping shape the town as a busy tea trading center. When local business was in its prime, in addition to the earliest and longest Tea-horse Route between Xizang and Yunnan, another route linking Yiwu with the Southeast Asian countries by way of Laos and Vietnam was opened. With the decline of the tea trade in late Qing Dynasty, these ancient trails were abandoned and dilapidated. Only the worn slates witness the past glory.

The warm and humid climate and abundant rainfall provide favorable conditions for tea to grow. Today, there are still plenty of tea plantations and the tea business active. The Seven-packed Tea Cake and Ingot-shaped Tea are the best-known local specialties. Back in the Qing Dynasty (1616-1911), the latter was selected as tribute tea to the royal family and traded throughout China, even to some Southeast Asian countries. One may still find well-preserved tea trees that once yielded fine leaves to make tribute tea.

- 易武镇"断案碑"

易武镇中心小学原是一座关圣庙的遗址，庙里墙上倚着一块石碑，记录着道光十六年（1836年）因茶税引出的一桩案件，故被人称为"断案碑"或"茶案碑"。这块石碑可以说是易武镇曾经兴旺的茶史的见证。

A Tea Case Stele at Yiwu Town

The Central Primary School of Yiwu Town stands on the former site of the Temple of Guan Yu. Beside the wall of the Temple stands a stele recording a tea-related tax case in the 16th year during the reign of Emperor Daoguang of the Qing Dynasty (1836). Known as the Tea-case Stele, it serves as a witness to the once thriving tea business in the town of Yiwu.

> 普洱茶的源头和集散地普洱

普洱市（原思茅市）位于云南省南部、澜沧江中下游，是滇藏茶马古道的源头，距今已有1800年

> Pu'er: Place of Origin and Distribution Center of Pu'er Tea

Situated in southern Yunnan Province and the lower middle reach of the Lancang River, the City of Pu'er, formerly known as Simao, has a history of about 1,800 years. Thanks to the subtropical monsoon climate, areas around the city are frost-free all year long. Thus Pu'er City has

- **镇沅镇千家寨的茶树王**

  生长在镇沅镇千家寨的千年茶树王树龄已有2700多年，是世界上已知的最古老的茶树。而澜沧邦崴的千年古茶树是世界上已知的唯一的过渡性大茶树，可以说是茶树从野生到人工种植这一进化过程的见证。

  The Tea Tree King at Qianjiazhai, Zhenyuan Town

  Growing in Qianjiazhai, Zhenyuan Town, this old Tea Tree is more than 2,700 years old. It is the oldest tea tree ever known in the world. There is another over 1,000 year old tea tree in Bangwei Village, Lancang County, Pu'er. It is the only known tea tree in a transitional stage, serving as an evidence of the domesticating of wild tea trees.

的历史。由于受亚热带季风气候的影响，这里大部分地区常年无霜，是著名的普洱茶的原产地和集散中心，曾经见证过普洱茶贸易的盛衰，也是中国最大的产茶区之一。普洱因茶而兴，雍正年间就因普洱茶的远销而繁荣，道光及光绪初年，这里商贾云集，市场繁荣，外地商旅纷纷落户。1917年起，普洱茶成为大宗出口商品，沿着以这里为起点的茶马古道，畅销各地，名扬四海。

普洱境内的运茶古道一般用青石铺成，宽约1米。在普洱城北，至今还保存有当年的茶庵塘古道。

become a famous place of origin and distribution center of Pu'er Tea. As one of the largest tea-growing areas in China, Pu'er city has witnessed tea rise and fall of the trade of Pu'er Tea. The growth of the city was driven by tea economy. Because of the popularity of Pu'er Tea, the City enjoyed a booming growth during the reign of Emperor Yongzheng of the Qing Dynasty, and attracted merchants coming afar during the reign of Emperor Daoguang and in the early years of the reign of Emperor Guangxu. Since 1917 when Pu'er Tea became a commodity for bulk export, the tea was shipped from the City to other parts of the world through the Ancient Tea-horse Road.

Within the city area, the road for transporting tea runs on a one-meter-wide pathway paved with slates. In the north part of the city, there is a well-preserved section of the Ancient Cha'antang Road, known as Cha'an Birds' Trail. Built in the Qing Dynasty, it was a government-invested official road for transporting the Pu'er Tea to the royal family. It starts from Pu'er City, runs northwards through Mohei Town, and ends in Kunming —

• 普洱境内的茶庵鸟道
Cha'an Birds' Trail, Pu'er City

它被称为"茶庵鸟道"，修建于清代，是为了向京城进贡普洱茶而建的官道，由普洱至磨黑镇以北直到省会昆明。这条驿道蜿蜒在崇山峻岭之中，长约5千米，石上已踏出了2厘米深的马蹄印，其历史之久远可见一斑。另外在普洱城南同心乡那柯里村南边，还保存着那柯里古道遗迹，它由人工磨制的条石和砾石铺成，路面宽1.5米，全长约有30千米。

capital of Yunnan Province. It winds through the mountains for about five kilometers. On this stone trail, one may still find two-centimeter deep hoof marks on the slates. In Nakeli Village, Tongxin Township, Pu'er City, there is another well-preserved section of the Ancient Tea-horse Road, Known as the Ancient Nakeli Road, this 1.5-meter wide road, paved with slates and gravels, extends about 30 kilometers intermittently.

• 普洱府旧址
Site of the Former Government Office of Pu'er Prefecture

> 古城大理

大理市是大理白族自治州的首府，地处云南省中部偏西，这里气候温和，土地肥沃，风光秀丽，是中国西南边疆开发较早的地区之一。远在四千多年前，大理就有原始居民活动。唐代初年，洱海地区"六诏"（唐初分布在洱海地区的六大少数民族部落）中的蒙舍诏势力渐强，在唐朝支持下，于开元二十六年（738年）统一"六诏"，建立了南诏国。南诏时期，大理地区的政治、经济、文化、生产技术等都有了长足的发展，享誉海内外的崇圣寺三塔就是当时的产物。公元937年，节度使段思平建立大理国，与中原宋王朝的关系更加密切，贸易频繁。

> Dali: A Beautiful Ancient Town

Situated in the west central area of Yunnan Province, Dali, capital of the Dali Bai Autonomous Prefecture, blessed with mild climate, fertile soil and beautiful landscapes, is one of the earliest-developed development areas in the southwestern frontier. Historical records show that as early as some 4,000 years ago, original inhabitants began to engage in production activities. In the early years of the Tang Dynasty, the Mengshe Tribe, one of the six main tribes living around the Erhai Lake areas grew stronger. Supported by the Tang-dynasty government, the Mengshe Tribe conquered all the other five tribes and established the Nanzhao Kingdom in the 26th year of the Kaiyuan Period of the Tang Dynasty(738). During the Nanzhao

• 大理苍山

苍山山顶的积雪经夏不消，在风和日丽的阳春三月更显得晶莹剔透，如同水晶世界。

Mount Cangshan, Dali City

Mount Cangshan has snow-capped peaks all the year anund, which glitter like crystals in sunny spring days.

大理的苍山洱海，是古今旅游者向往的地方。苍山，又名点苍山，共有19座山峰，每座山峰海拔都在3500米以上。洱海是一个风光明媚的高原湖泊，呈狭长形，那干净透明的水面宛如碧澄的蓝天，给人以宁静悠远的感觉。在苍山脚下、洱海之滨，还有遐迩闻名的蝴蝶泉。每年农历三四月间，成千上万的蝴蝶从四面八方飞来，在泉边漫天飞舞，五彩斑斓，如霞如锦，蔚为奇观。

Kingdom Period, Dali experienced a rapid growth politically, economically, culturally and technically. The famous Three Pagodas (of Chongsheng Temple) were built during this period. In 937, local governor Duan Siping founded the Dali Kingdom and fostered a closer tie with the central government of the Song Dynasty, which led to more frequent trade between Dali and the Central Plains.

Mount Cangshan and Erhai Lake have been the most desired tourist

● 大理白族女孩
A Bai Girl of Dali City

古城大理是茶马古道的重要枢纽。大理茶马古道中原貌保持最好的一段位于凤阳邑。这段古道全长700余米，路宽2.6—3.2米，当中铺长1米、宽0.6米左右的条石，即"引马石"，两侧各铺宽约15厘米的卵石道，道旁为石凳，具有典型的茶马古道特征。古道周边为古老的白族民居，墙体为不规则的石头所砌，独具特色。古道两边为石凳和铺台子，还有茶铺。铺台子为石头所砌，简朴粗犷。茶铺简单却具有民族风味。石凳、铺台子和茶铺为过往的商客提供补给和休

destinations in Dali. While Mount Cangshan has 19 peaks over 3,500 meters above sea level, Erhai Lake is a beautiful long and narrow plateau lake where clean and serene water colors like the blue sky. At the foot of Mount Cangshan and by the Erhai Lake, there is a well-known Butter y Spring, which attracts, between the third and fourth months of the Chinese lunar calendar, thousands of butterflies dancing around, making a spectacular scene.

The Ancient Town of Dali is an important hub on the Ancient Tea-horse Road. One may find the best preserved section of the Road in Fengyangyi. Over 700 meters long and 2.6 to 3.2 meters wide, this Road was paved with slates of 1 meter long, 0.6 meter wide known as the "Bridle Stones" in the middle and 15-centimeter wide gravel on both sides. Along the Ancient Road, there stand many ancient Bai houses with walls built with irregular stones in unique patterns. There are stone tables and stools and small shops for caravans and travelers to take a break and get some supplies. All these elements

息，是茶马古道特有的风采，石头文化也独具魅力。古道边上有水井，为过往客商和本地居民提供可以饮用的水。

constitute a unique scene on the Ancient Road. Moreover, there are also wells along the Road, providing drinking water to travelers as well as local residents.

- **大理崇圣寺三塔**

  崇圣寺三塔，位于大理古城北的苍山脚下。崇圣寺是初建于南诏丰佑年间的佛教寺院，现庙宇建筑已毁，只有三塔完好地保留下来，成为文化名城大理的象征。

  The Three Pagodas at Chongsheng Temple, Dali

  The Three Pagodas at the Chongsheng Temple stand at the foot of Mount Cangshan north of the Ancient Dali Town. Built in the Fengyou Period (824-859) of the Nanzhao Kingdom, the Chongsheng Temple was a Buddhist temple. As the only surviving buildings of the temple, the Three Pagodas have become a cultural symbol of Dali.

大理下关沱茶

据史料记载，清代末年，云南茶叶集散市场逐渐转移到交通方便、工商业发达的大理下关。而下关的永昌祥、复春和等茶号的茶商创制了碗状沱茶，经昆明运往重庆、成都等地销售。下关沱茶选用云南省临沧、保山、思茅等30多地出产的茶叶为原料，经过人工揉制、机器压紧数道工序制作而成，形如碗状，造型优美，色泽乌润显毫，香气清纯馥郁，汤色橙黄清亮，滋味醇爽回甘。依原料不同，沱茶有绿茶沱茶和黑茶沱茶之分。绿茶沱茶是以较细嫩的晒青绿毛茶为原料，经蒸压而制成，称云南沱茶；黑茶沱茶是以普洱茶为原料，经蒸压而制成，称云南普洱沱茶。

Bowl-shaped Tea of Xiaguan, Dali

According to historical records, in late Qing Dynasty, the tea distribution center in Yunnan gradually shifted to Xiaguan, Dali, where transportation was more convenient and local commerce and industry were more developed. Local tea manufacturers, e.g. *Yongchangxiang* and *Fuchunhe*, created bowl-shaped compressed tea "*Tuocha*", and shipped them out via Kunming and sold them to Sichuan (Chongqing, Chengdu and other places). Made of primary tea from more than thirty areas in Yunnan (including Lincang, Baoshan, and Simao) after a simple process (physical rolling by hand and mechanical compression), these cute bowl-shaped tea blocks have a dark appearance and pure and refreshing aroma and make clear, orange infusions. Bowl-shaped Tea can be categorized into green Bowl-shaped Tea and black Bowl-shaped Tea according to the primary tea. The former, known as Bowl-shaped Tea of Yunnan Province, is made of fine, dried green primary tea after steaming and compression molding; whereas, the latter, known as Pu'er Bowl-shaped Tea of Yunnan Province is made of Pu'er Tea after a steaming and compression molding process.

• 20世纪50年代中期生产的下关沱茶
Bowl-shaped Tea of Xiaguan Town Made in the Mid-1950s

> 土司故地丽江

丽江古城位于云南省丽江市古城区，是一个纳西族、汉族、白族、傈僳族、彝族、苗族等多

> Lijiang: Former Residence of Aboriginal Office

Situated in the Lijiang, Yunnan Province, the Ancient Town of Lijiang is of historic and cultural meaning as well as home

- 玉龙雪山下的丽江古城
  The Ancient Town of Lijiang at the Foot of the Jade Loong Snow Mountain

• 丽江城里的纳西族老人
Two Naxi Elderly women in the Town of Lijiang

民族杂居的古城，也是一座历史文化名城。早在南宋时期，丽江古城就已初具规模，至今已有八九百年的历史。明代末年，丽江在木氏土司的统治下日渐繁荣，土司所营造的土司府非常华美，明代旅行家徐霞客在游记中称其"宫室之丽，拟于王者"。

丽江地处青藏高原南端山峡耸峙的横断山脉，东与四川毗邻，北同西藏接壤，是云南通往西藏的必经之地，也是滇藏茶马古道的唯一通道。明清以来，地处茶马古道要冲的丽江成为茶马古道上来往马

to many ethnic groups including Naxi, Han, Bai, Lisu, Yi, Miao and others. The town began to take shape as early as the Southern Song Dynasty and has a history of about 800 or 900 years. Entering the late Ming Dynasty, the town prospered under the rule of the Aboriginal Office of the Mu family. The chieftain's residence was splendid. Xu Xiake, a traveler of the Ming Dynasty, once noted that this magnificent residence may rival a king's palace.

Nestled in the Hengduan Mountains in the southern end of the Qinghai-Xizang Plateau and adjacent to Sichuan in the east and Xizang in the north, Lijiang is on the only passage between Yunnan and Xizang. During the Ming and Qing dynasties, caravans and merchants on the Ancient Tea-horse Road stopped here to take a rest. Hence, it is said that Lijiang was built by the treading hoofs of caravans.

During the Qing Dynasty, as the Han-Zang trade grew along the Ancient Tea-horse Road, Lijiang accommodated a developed commercial and trade

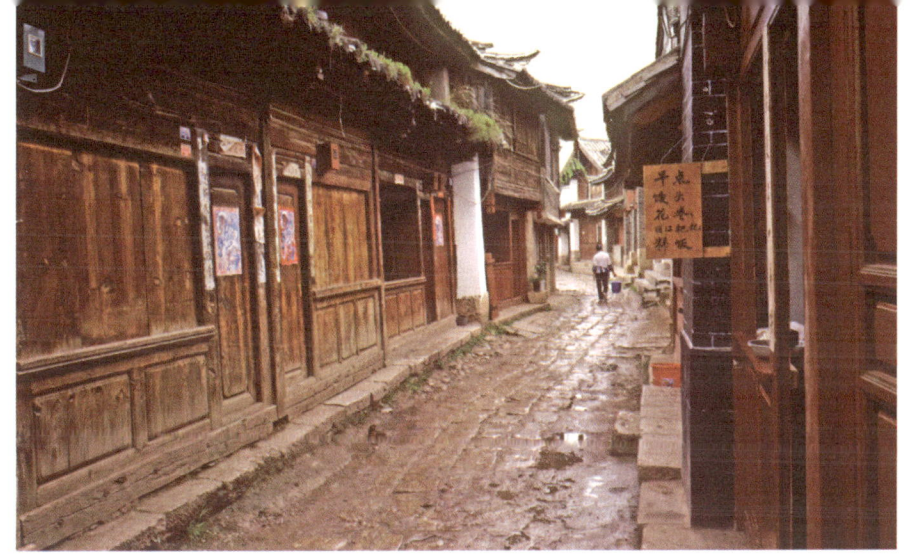

• 丽江古城的石板街道
A Slate Street in the Ancient Town of Lijiang

帮、客商歇脚和打尖的地方，所以有人说，丽江是一座由马蹄踏出来的古城。

清代，随着以茶马古道为主线的汉藏贸易的日渐繁荣，丽江的商贸市场已有相当规模，并成为"雇脚转运"货物到藏族聚居区的商贸中转站。丽江丰富多样的文化习俗、生活方式和多种语言的通用，使来自山南海北的商家感到方便，再加上四季宜人的气候，很多内地的商人到了丽江就驻足不前，将此地作为生意的基地。来自内地的各种货物、邻近地区的土特产品等，多再由熟悉藏族聚居区的丽江商人集中运到藏族聚居区，藏族商人将

market and functioned like a transit depot for porters. The town embraced diverse culture, customs, lifestyles and languages. People understood, appreciated and lived in peace with each other. Merchants felt welcomed and found it convenient to do business here. Moreover, the pleasant weather in all seasons appealed to business people from the Central Plains. Many made Lijiang their business base and conducted transactions locally. Goods from the Central Plains and specialties from surrounding areas were purchased and shipped in bulk by local businessmen to the areas inhabited by Zang people, and Zang merchants did the same. They carried their goods to

藏地的土特产品运到丽江后，也不再继续南下，而是就地进行交易。在清代，丽江的纳西人中逐渐产生了专门从事茶马古道进藏贸易的"藏客"——到西藏进行贸易的纳西商家。清末民初，丽江古城当藏客的纳西人逐渐增多，他们自己成立马帮进藏族聚居区做生意，成为茶马古道上的客商。

Lijiang and traded here, instead of going further south. In the Qing Dynasty, some local Naxi people became merchants travelling on the Ancient Tea-horse Road to trade with Zang people. During the late Qing Dynasty and early years of the Minguo Period, these merchants increased in number and many set up their own caravans.

- 丽江木氏土司府

  纳西族最高统领木氏自元代世袭丽江土司以来,历经元、明、清三代,22世470年。木府在明末时达到鼎盛,位于丽江古城西南隅,占地一百多亩,有近百座建筑,建筑气象万千。

  Aboriginal Office of the Mu Family, Lijiang City

  Having received the hereditary title as Aboriginal Office of Lijiang during the Yuan Dynasty, the Mu family, the chief family of Naxi people, ruled the area for 22 generations or 470 years through the Yuan, Ming, and Qing dynasties. The Mu Residence was at its prime time during the late Ming Dynasty. Covering an area of more than 7 hectares in the southwest corner of the Town, the estate consisted of nearly one hundred magnificent buildings of grand architectural style.

> 人间仙境香格里拉

> Shangr-La: Paradise on Earth

香格里拉是云南省迪庆藏族自治州的首府所在地，原名"中甸"，地处青藏高原南缘，市政府

Lying at the southern edge of the Qinghai-Xizang Plateau, Shangri-La City, formerly known as Zhongdian, is the capital of the Diqing Zang Autonomous

- 纳帕海

纳帕海是一个美丽的季节性高原湖泊，位于香格里拉西北部。这里三面环山，许多珍禽栖息于此。纳帕海周围的草甸面积达30平方千米，远山、湖泊、草场、牛羊，组成了迷人的草原美景。

Napa Sea

Napa Sea is a beautiful seasonal highland lake, located in the northwestern part of Shangri-La. Flanked on three sides by mountains, it is the habitat of many rare birds. The lake is surrounded by a vast meadow of over 30 square kilometers. The distant mountains, the lake ripples, the pastures, cattle and sheep constitute a charming grassland beauty.

所在地建塘镇已有1300多年的历史，曾是茶马古道上的重要驿站和进入藏族聚居区的交通要隘，海拔超过3300米。

香格里拉市境内海拔4000米以上的雪山就达470座，峡谷纵横深邃，最著名的有金沙江虎跳峡、澜沧江峡谷等，还有辽阔的高山草原牧场、莽莽的原始森林，以及星罗棋布的高山湖泊，自然景观神奇

- 香格里拉风光
  The Beautiful Scenery of Shangri-La City

Prefecture, Yunnan Province. With a history of more than 1,300 years and situated on the highland of 3,300 meters elevation, Jiantang Town, seat of the city government, was an important post on the Ancient Tea-horse Road as well as a strategic gateway into the areas inhabited by Zang people.

Within Shangri-La City, there are 470 snow-capped mountains of over 4,000 meters elevation and many deep canyons. The most famous ones include the Tiger Leaping Gorge on the Jinsha

● 松赞林寺

松赞林寺是云南藏族聚居区藏传佛教寺院，初建于1681年。寺中的主要建筑扎仓、吉康两座大殿高高矗立在中央，其余建筑簇拥拱卫，高低错落，层层递进，体现出藏式佛教建筑恢弘、辉煌的特色。

Songzanlin Temple

Built in 1681, Songzanlin is the most famous Zang Buddhist temple in Yunnan Province. In the middle of the temple complex stand two imposing halls named Zhacang and Jikang. Other buildings are carefully arranged around the two main buildings, displaying the magnificence and grandeur of Zang Buddhist architecture.

险峻而又清幽灵秀。这里还生活着藏族、傈僳族、汉族、纳西族、彝族、白族、回族等13个民族,他们相处和睦,在生活方式、服饰、民居建筑以及婚俗礼仪等传统习俗中,都保持了本民族的特色,形成了各民族独特的风情。无垠的草甸、辉煌的寺庙、历史悠久的宗教文化、多姿多彩的民族风情,使香格里拉被中外游客视为心中的世外桃源。

River and the Grand Canyon of the Lancang River. The city also featured vast alpine pastures, virgin forests and dotted mountain lakes. The natural landscape is stunningly precipitous, serene and beautiful. The city is home to some thirteen ethnic groups, including Zang, Lisu, Han, Naxi, Yi, Bai, Hui, etc. They live in peace and harmony while maintaining their own customs and traditions in terms of life style, clothing, architecture, wedding traditions and others. The boundless meadows, splendid monasteries, ancient culture of religion, colorful ethnic customs make Shangri-La the land of idyllic beauty in the eyes of domestic and international tourists.

香格里拉的由来

"香格里拉"在藏语中意为"心中的日月",是佛教传说中的净土和理想王国,也被称为"香巴拉"。英国作家詹姆斯·希尔顿1933年出版的小说《消失的地平线》中描绘了一个叫"香格里拉"的地方,那里有澄碧的蓝天、漫山开放的杜鹃和神秘幽静的藏传佛教寺院,远处的雪山熠熠生辉。由于这部小说,"香格里拉"一词成为人间乐园和世外桃源的代名词。后来有心人发现,迪庆中甸的自然与人文景观竟然与书中描绘的"香格里拉"的景观惊人地相似,而且中甸古城的藏语地名也叫"香格里拉"。更神奇的是,詹姆斯·希尔顿一生从未到过中国,更不可能知道中甸这个地方。2001年,中甸县正式改名为香格里拉市。

History of Shangri-La

In the Zang language, Shangri-La means "the sun and the moon in the heart". The place is also known as Shambhala — the pure land and paradise in Buddhist legends. In his novel the *Lost Horizon* (1933), English writer James Hilton depicted a place called Shangri-La where the sky is clear blue, azalea blooms abound, snow-capped mountains glitter in the distance and a mysterious secluded Zang Buddhist temple is seated. After the novel was published, Shangri-La became a synonym for paradise on earth and the land of idyllic beauty. Later, some sharp-eyed people discovered that the natural and cultural landscape of Zhongdian County, Diqing Zang Autonomous Prefecture showed many similarities to what were described in Hilton's book. And the ancient town of Zhongdian was also called Shangri-La in the Zang language. What was even more amazing was that people found that Mr. Hilton had never been to China during his life time, let alone knew about Zhongdian. In 2001, the county was officially renamed Shangri-La.

- 传说中的世外桃源香格里拉
  Shangri-La: the Legendary Land of Idyllic Paradise on Earth

> 雪山集市德钦

德钦县位于云南省迪庆藏族自治州西北部，地处青藏高原的南缘部分，横断山脉中段，"三江并流"腹地。德钦县境内有气势磅礴、巍峨耸峙的梅里雪山，有美丽迷人的高山湖泊和草甸，还有金碧辉煌的寺院和神秘的藏传佛教文化，生活在这里的各民族都有自己独特的民族服饰、习俗、节日、手工艺，展现出多姿多彩的民族风情。

德钦县政府所在的升平镇，是云南省境内最北端和海拔最高的城镇，自唐宋以来就是茶马互市的重要通道。来自云南大理、丽江和西藏、四川、青海、甘肃的商人都在这里设立商号。尤其是在抗战时

> Deqin: A Market in Snow Mountains

Situated in the northwest of the Diqing Zang Autonomous Prefecture, Yunnan Province, the Deqin County is on the southern outreach of the Qinghai-Xizang Plateau, the middle part of the Hengduan Mountains, and the hinterland of the Three Parallel Rivers. The landscape of the county features imposing Meili Snow Mountains, beautiful alpine lakes and meadows, magnificent monasteries and mysterious Zang Buddhism culture. Ethnic groups living here all have their own traditions in terms of clothing, customs, festivals and handicrafts, displaying a diverse and dazzling ethnic cultural environment.

Shengping Town, county seat of Deqin, is a town at the northernmost point of Yunnan with the highest

期，这里成为重要的物资运输口岸，曾经十分繁荣，被马帮称为"小上海"。小镇四面环山，地势陡峭，镇内建筑依山而建，呈梯形分布，

● **金沙江畔的奔子栏村**

奔子栏村位于德钦县南部的金沙江西岸，是滇藏茶马古道的咽喉之地。村民信仰藏传佛教，村寨基本保持着传统风貌，宗教文化色彩十分浓厚。

The Benzilan Village by the Jinsha River

Situated on the west bank of the Jinsha River in the south of Deqin County, the Benzilan Village holds an important position on the Ancient Tea-horse Road from Yunnan to Xizang. Local residents believe in Xizang Buddhism and maintain their residences in a traditional style dominated by the religious culture.

elevation. The town has been an important post for the Tea-horse Trade since the Tang and Song (960-1279) dynasties. Many business people from Dali and Lijiang of Yunnan, Xizang, Sichuan, Qinghai, and Gansu set up operations in Shengping. During the War of Resistance against Japanese Invasion, Shengping served as a port of entry for freight transportation. Hence it was nicknamed the mini-Shanghai by caravans. Surrounded by mountains, the town is built in a terraced arrangement

显得较为拥挤。每年秋末冬初，镇上云雾弥漫，有时雾气飘入民房，被当地人称为"天香熏室"。

on a steep terrain and seems rather crowded. Between late autumn and early winter each year, dense fog envelops the town and sometimes pervades into houses and rooms. Local residents refer to this natural phenomenon as Incense from Heaven.

- **雄伟的梅里雪山**

梅里雪山是云南最壮观的雪山群，梅里雪山以其巍峨壮丽、神秘莫测而闻名于世。数百里兀立绵延的雪岭雪峰，占去德钦县34.5%的面积。主峰卡瓦格博峰海拔6740米，是云南最高的山峰。藏族人认为，每一座高山的山神统领一方自然，梅里雪山的主峰卡瓦格博峰则被尊奉为藏传佛教的八大神山之首。

The Magnificent Meili Snow Mountains

The Meili Snow Mountain range has the most spectacular snow-capped peaks in Yunnan known for its majestic beauty and unfathomable mystery. These imposing snow-capped mountain ranges stretch for hundreds of miles, covering an area as much as 34.5% of the Deqin County territory. Its main peak—the Kawagebo Peak, has an altitude of 6,740 meters and is the highest peak in Yunnan. Zang people believe that in every high mountain resides a god who takes control of the nature of the land around and the Kawagebo Peak is regarded as the most important mountain peak among the eight holy mountains in Zang Buddhism.

三江并流

　　"三江并流"是指金沙江、澜沧江和怒江这三条发源于青藏高原的大江在云南省境内自北向南并行奔流170多千米，穿越担当力卡山、高黎贡山、怒山和云岭等崇山峻岭，形成罕见的"江水并流而不交汇"的奇特景观。其间澜沧江与金沙江最短直线距离为66千米，澜沧江与怒江的最短直线距离不到19千米。

The Three Parallel Rivers

The Three Parallel Rivers refer to the Jinsha, Lancang and Nujiang rivers, all originated in the Qinghai-Xizang Plateau, running through Yunnan Province side by side from north to south for over 170 kilometers. While they surge through the high mountains of Dandanglika, Gaoligong, Nushan, Yunling and others, they each follow their own course, making a spectacular landscape where rivers run side-by-side without converging. The Lancang River is only 66 kilometers apart from the Jinsha River and less than 19 kilometers from the Nujiang River at the closest points.

● **金沙江大转弯** (图片提供: FOTOE)

金沙江大转弯也叫"月亮湾"，位于云南德钦县奔子栏镇和四川得荣县了庚乡交界处。奔腾而来的金沙江，在此绕着金字塔形的日锥峰画下了一个"Ω"形的大拐弯，形成了一个神奇雄壮的奇景。

The Big Bend of the Jinsha River

The Big Bend of the Jinsha River, also known as the Moon Bay, lies at the border between Benzilan Town of Deqin County, Yunnan Province and Zigeng Village of Derong County, Sichuan Province. Around the pyramid-like Rizhui Peak, the River takes a big Ω-shaped turn and creates an amazing sight of wonder.

古道驿镇 / Towns on the Ancient Tea-horse Road

> 边茶产地雅安

　　雅安位于四川省中部，成都平原与青藏高原的过渡带，自古就是川、藏、滇三省（区）的交通咽喉与川藏民间贸易的商品集散地。雅安是川藏南路茶马古道的起始地，雅安名山区境内的蒙顶山在唐代

> Ya'an: Place of Origin of Border Tea

Situated in the center of Sichuan Province in the transitional slope area between the Chengdu Plain and the Qinghai-Xizang Plateau, Ya'an has been an important transportation thoroughfare between Sichuan, Xizang and Yunnan, and the distribution center for domestic trade between Sichuan and Xizang since ancient times. As the starting point of the southern route of the Ancient Tea-horse Road, tea was first shipped from Ya'an to Xizang for trade. Since the Tang

• 蒙顶山茶园
　A Tea Plantation at Mount Mengding

清代茶马司旧址
Site of the Former Tea and Horse Trade Authority Office of the Qing Dynasty

就以出产蒙顶茶著称。宋代，蒙顶茶成为茶马贸易的专用商品。宋代在雅安设置"茶马互市司"，专门管理茶马互市事宜。清道光二十九年（1849年），朝廷重修茶马司，对内地和藏族聚居区的贸易交流起到了推动作用。鼎盛时期，这里的边茶贸易量达到"岁运名山茶二万驮"之多，有时一日接待商人达2000余人。蒙顶茶通过茶马古道输入藏族聚居区，是历代中央政府与藏、羌等少数民族进行茶马贸易的专用商品，成为汉族人民同藏、羌等各族人民增强政治、经济、文化

Dynasty, Mount Mengding in Mingshan County, Ya'an has been known for its local product, Mengding Tea. In the Song Dynasty, the government set up a Tea and Horse Trade Authority in Ya'an. And in the 29th year during the reign of Emperor Daoguang of the Qing Dynasty (1849), the government reinstituted the Authority, helping promote trade and exchanges between the Central Plains and the areas inhabited by Zang people. In its heydays, the City's Border Tea trade volume reached 20,000 loads of pack horses a year. Sometimes the city had to accommodate more than 2,000 men in a single day. Shipped to the areas inhabited by Zang people through the Ancient Tea-horse Road, Mengding Tea trade was, for many dynasties, a gentral government monopoly. Indeed Mengding Tea had been a linkage between the Han people and ethnic groups in terms of cultural, economic and political exchanges. "Tea from Mount Mengding with water from the Yangtze River makes a good cup of tea". For thousands of years, Mengding Tea has been enjoying a prestigious reputation for its fine quality, special status and refined production process.

Ancient towns of Shangli and Wangyu of Ya'an are two important towns

交流的重要纽带。"扬子江中水，蒙山顶上茶"，千百年来蒙顶茶以优异的品质、特殊的地位、精湛的制作工艺享誉于世。

雅安的上里古镇和望鱼古镇均是茶马古道上的重镇，依山傍水，田园小丘，木屋为舍，现仍保留着许多明清风貌的吊脚楼式建筑和文物古迹，是品茗、咏史难得的胜迹。

on the Ancient Tea-horse Road. Both are situated by a river at the foot of a mountain and have fields and houses among hills. There remain old stilted houses and historical architectural sites, allowing people today to learn about history while enjoying a cup of aromatic tea.

蒙顶茶

蒙顶茶，产于地横跨四川省雅安市名山、雨城两区的蒙顶山，是蒙山顶所产各种花色名茶的统称，其中品质最佳的有"蒙顶甘露""蒙顶黄芽"等，其品质特点为外形美观，香气高爽，味醇甘鲜，汤黄微碧，清澈明亮。从唐代起，蒙顶茶就被列入贡茶，直到清代灭亡。宋代是蒙顶茶发展的极盛时期，蒙顶茶的质量有很大提高，制茶技艺进一步完善，创制出万春银叶、玉叶长春等贡茶。那时，四川茶叶产量居全国第一，而蒙顶茶产量又居四川之首。而且蒙顶茶受到西南、西北地区少数民族的喜爱，朝廷曾特诏"专以雅州名山茶易马，不得他用"。

Mengding Tea

Mengding Tea is the generic name of tea varieties grown in Mount Mengding at Mingshan and Yucheng districts, Ya'an City, Sichuan Province. The best quality tea varieties include the Mengding Dew (*Mengding Ganlu*) and Mengding Yellow Buds (*Mengding Huangya*). They have refreshing aroma and make bright, clear, greenish yellow tea water with a pure, sweet taste. Since the Tang Dynasty, Mengding tea was designated as tribute tea to the royal family, a tradition lasted until the end of the Qing Dynasty. Mengding Tea's golden age came during the Song Dynasty when the production process was further refined and the quality improved.

New tea varieties including Ten Thousand Spring Silver Leaves (*Wanchun Yinye*) and Jade Leaf Eternal Spring (*Yuye Changchun*) were created and added to the list of tribute tea. Back then, Sichuan topped all the other provinces in tea output and Mount Mengding topped all the other tea-growing areas in Sichuan. Mengding Tea was also among the favorites of ethnic groups in Southwest and Northwest China. And the government issued a special order that tea from Mount Mingshan, Ya'an be used for trading horses only.

- 历代名茶蒙顶黄芽
  Mengding Yellow Buds (*Mengding Huangya*)—A Famous Tea Variety Since Ancient Times

> 锅庄之城康定

康定市，旧称"打箭炉"，位于川西贡嘎山北端的跑马山麓，是甘孜藏族自治州首府，也是一座历史悠久的高原古城。作为茶马古道上的历史文化名城，康定坐落在三山两水之间的河谷地带，藏语称康定为"打折多"，意为打曲（雅

> Kangding: Town of Wok Stands (*Guozhuang*)

Lying at the foothills of Mount Paoma at the northern end of Mount Gongga in western Sichuan, and formerly known as Dajianlu, Kangding is the capital of the Ganzi Zang Autonomous Prefecture, as well as a historical city on the Qinghai-Xizang Plateau. As an ancient cultural city on the Tea-horse Road, Kangding lies in the valley surrounded by three mountains and two rivers. The name of the city in Zang language means the confluence of two rivers. The city had changed its name several times and had been known as the "Town of Wok Stands" before adopting the current official name of Kangding.

- 康定城俯瞰
  A Bird's-eye View of Kangding

拉河)、折曲(折多河)两河交汇处,旧史曾译作"打煎炉",后通译"打箭炉",简称"炉城"。

打箭炉在元代尚为荒凉的山沟,明代开碉门、岩州茶马道后,逐渐成为大渡河以西各驮队集散之地。清康熙三十二年(1693年),达赖喇嘛奏请打箭炉"交市之事",三十五年(1696年),康熙准"行打箭炉市,蕃人市茶贸易"。这一纸皇命改变了康定的命运,使康定后来成为茶马古道上的枢纽、繁华的西陲重镇、藏汉物资文化交流中心和西南最大的物资集散地,商业繁荣昌盛。20世纪30年代,康定已成为闻名于世的藏汉贸易的中心,是与上海、武汉齐名的三大商埠之一。

康定以其特有的锅庄文化闻名于世。大渡河上游康定、丹巴一带藏族的家家户户都有一间客厅兼厨房的大屋子,称为"锅庄"。由于屋子里大火塘中有用三根石头打制的支锅柱,专为熬茶做饭时放锅,故这间屋子也被称为"锅庄"。康定的锅庄应该是从第一支茶马古道的商队在这里燃起第一把火、支起第一个熬茶的"锅桩"时就开始

Dajianlu, still a desolate valley during the Yuan Dynasty, grew into a caravan distribution center west of the Dadu River after the Tea-horse Road between Diaomen and Yanzhou was built in the Ming Dynasty. In the 32nd year during the reign of Emperor Kangxi of the Qing Dynasty (1693), the then Dalai Lama submitted a memorial to emperor concerning the issue of a trade market at Dajianlu. Later in the 35th year (1696), the Emperor endorsed the proposal for the establishment of Dajianlu Township to facilitate trade with Zang people, a decision that changed the fate of the area completely. The township became a hub on the Ancient Tea-horse Road, a prosperous major trading town on the western frontier, a trade and cultural exchange center between Han people and Zang people, and the largest goods distribution center in the southwest region. Local commerce was thriving. In the 1930s, the town was widely known as Han and Zang trade center, one of the three famous commercial centers at the time, comparable to Shanghai and Wuhan.

Kangding is also known for the local *Guozhuang* culture. In Kangding city and Danba County on the upper reach of

• 康定新都桥镇风光

新都桥位于康定市境内，是川藏公路上的一个小镇，是从康定通往西藏的必经之地。这里景色如诗如画，被誉为"光与影的世界""摄影家的天堂"。

Xinduqiao Town, Kangding City

Xinduqiao, a small town under the administration of Kangding City, is on the Sichuan-Xizang Highway, the only access from Kangding to Xizang. With its amazing landscape and poetic scenery, this town is known as the "world of lights and shadows" and the "paradise for photographers".

了。然而随着历史的发展，康定的锅庄早已从支锅熬茶的"锅桩"里脱胎出来，变成一种专供茶马贸易的康定独有的机构。在康定的茶马贸易中，锅庄扮演了十分活跃的角色，它既是供过往茶商和驮队食宿之地，又是贸易的中介处。藏地的药材、羊毛、皮张和黄金等土特产品与来自内地的边茶、绸缎、粮食等生产生活用品云集康定，均堆放于锅庄中。藏、汉、回等各族商人在锅庄主人的中介下互市，生意兴

the Dadu River, Zang people had a large room serving as the living room and the kitchen. This room is called *Guozhuang* (literally means wok stands). There was usually a large fireplace where three stone pillars were erected to support a pot or a wok for boiling tea or cooking meals. Perhaps Kangding's *Guozhuang* culture started with the first fire lit by the first caravan member travelling on the Ancient Tea-horse Road to cook tea. However, with the advancement of history, *Guozhuang* transformed completely from

隆。在交易中，藏商销售土特产和购买茶叶等活动，均委托锅庄主人与汉商洽谈，成交后锅庄主人按总金额收2%—4%的佣金。康定茶商要争取买主，往往要千方百计地巴结锅庄主人，没有锅庄主人的牵头，茶商将一筹莫展。让人不可思议的是，担当这种"中间人"的多为锅庄里年轻漂亮、精明能干的女子，当地人叫她们"沙鸨"或"阿加"。这就构成茶商与锅庄的密切联系，有的甚至互相通婚，建立姻亲联系。

a stone-pillared fireplace for cooking to a unique venue and institution for Tea-horse trade. The host of *Guozhuang* provided caravans with accommodation and catering, and played the role of an intermediary. Local specialties shipped from Xizang, such as herbs, wool, furs and gold, and goods from the interior like Border Tea, silk, grain, household goods, and production tools were all stored in *Guozhuang* where Zang, Han, Hui and other ethnic merchants traded with each other with the help of the host. Most Zang merchants entrusted *Guozhuang* hosts with their sales and purchases and paid 2%-4% of the total sales income as commission to the host. To sell their products, tea merchants worked hard to ingratiate these intermediaries. For without their help, there would be no business. What was intriguing was that most of the intermediaries in *Guozhuang* were young, pretty and smart women, locally referred to as *Shabao* or *Ajia*. Hence, tea merchants all tried to develop an intimate relationship with *Guozhuang*, sometimes through marriage.

- 20世纪30年代的康定城东关城门"康定门"
  (图片提供：FOTOE)

Kangding Gate—the East Gate of the Ancient Town of Kangding in the 1930s

康定城的缝包工

边茶从雅安由脚夫扛运到康定，再向西行，山高路远，必须改为马运牛驮。从人背改为牛驮，茶厂简单的竹篾包装就不能适应需要，必须在外面再加上牛皮外套，使其更加坚固耐磨，于是在康定一种专门用牛皮重新包装茶叶的缝包工便应运而生了。缝包的工具相当简单，一把割牛皮用的刀，两根缝皮子用的钢针。包裹茶包用的牛皮需要在水中浸泡一周左右，湿润柔软后，才能使用。一个强壮的缝包工一天能缝制七八张牛皮，一张牛皮能装二三件竹茶包，缝好后的牛皮茶包还要放在太阳下晒一段时日才能运走。所以一支商队来到康定，互市交易可能很快完成，但要等待茶包缝入牛皮，往往要耽搁一个多月的时间才能踏上归途。由于康定的缝包工手艺出众，在藏族聚居区都很有影响，不论在什么地方，只要一提起康定的缝包工，没有一个茶商不竖大拇指。

● 装茶用的皮袋
A Leather Bag for Holding Tea

Bag Tailers in Kangding

Border Tea was carried by porters from Ya'an to Kangding and then by pack horses or yaks further to the west. Before being loaded onto the animals, leather wrapping was fitted around to the original bamboo basket, to provide additional wear-resistant protection. Hence in Kangding, a special-skilled profession, tea bag tailors emerged. They used simple tools, including a leather-cutting knife, two sewing needles, and cattle hide, which had to be soaked in water for about a week to make it soft and moist. A skilled, and strong bag tailor could make seven or eight hides per day, one hide could wrap two or three bales of tea in bamboo packaging. As finished leather bags needed to be exposed to sunlight for several days to get dry, it usually took more than one month for a caravan coming to Kangding to proceed on their return journey, though they might have closed the deals soon after they arrived. Local bag tailors enjoyed quite a reputation among tea merchants for their fine craftsmanship.

> "最后的净土"稻城

稻城县位于四川省西南边缘，地处青藏高原东南部，横断山脉东侧，属康巴藏族聚居区的甘孜藏族

> Daocheng: "The Last Pure Land on Earth"

Located on the eastern hillside of the Hengduan Mountains on the southeastern part of the Qinghai-Xizang Plateau,

• 稻城风光
A Landscape Picture of Daocheng County

自治州。稻城古名"稻坝"，藏语意为"山谷沟口开阔之地"。稻城是一个藏族聚居县，人口大多为藏族，他们的生活与自然融为一体，无论是服

Daocheng County is under the jurisdiction of the Ganzi Zang Autonomous Prefecture. In ancient times, it was known as Daoba, meaning an open land at the entrance of

- 亚丁风景区的神山仙乃日

亚丁风景区位于稻城东南面，以仙乃日、降边央、夏纳多吉三座雪峰为核心区，北南向分布。由于特殊的地理环境和自然气候，形成了独特的地貌和自然景观，被国际友人誉为"水蓝色星球上的最后一片净土"。

Divine Peak Xiannairi, Yading Scenic Area

Located in the southeast of Daocheng, Yading Scenic Area stretches from the north to the south and centers around three snow-capped peaks, i.e. Xiannairi, Jiangbianyang and Xianaduoji. The special geography and the climate shaped the unique terrain and landscape of the region, which has been referred to by tourists as "the last patch of pure land on this water-blue planet".

饰、建筑，还是习俗、歌舞，都取诸自然，顺应自然，自由自在。

  这里最高海拔达6032米，属高原季风气候，绝大多数时间天气晴朗，阳光明媚，自然风光优美，尤以古冰体遗迹"稻城古冰帽"著称于世。在稻城极目远眺，天地浩瀚无垠，乱石比比皆是，1000多个高山湖泊散落于嶙峋乱石间，景色极为壮观。

the valley in Zang language. Zang people comprise most of Daocheng's resident population. They live in harmony with nature in every aspect of their life: clothing, architecture, customs, songs and dances.

  The county has the highest elevation of 6,032 meters. It has a plateau monsoon climate and is sunny most of the time. Local landscapes are breathtaking, especially, the famous icecap — the landscape carved out by ancient glaciers. Underneath the firmament is a borderless world of rugged rocks dotted with more than 1,000 alpine lakes.

- 亚丁高山湖泊
  An Alpine Lake at Yading

> 交通咽喉泸定

泸定县位于四川省甘孜藏族自治州东南部，贡嘎山东坡、二郎山西麓，大渡河由北向南贯穿县境，是古代通往藏族聚居区的川藏古道必经之地。这里本是大渡河的重要渡口，两岸用竹绳索连接，赶马人与来往客商只能滑索而过。冬季枯水期，则坐用牛皮制成的船渡河。清康熙四十四年（1705年），康熙皇帝因军事需要及为了方便藏汉贸易下旨修建泸定铁索桥，并御笔亲题桥名"泸定桥"。

泸定桥建成后，成为四川内地通往青藏高原的重要通道，也是茶马古道上的交通咽喉。从此，马帮和脚夫再也不用冒着生命危险乘木船渡过水深浪急的大渡河了。而

> Luding: A Transportation Hub

Located in the southeastern part of the Ganzi Zang Autonomous Prefecture, Sichuan Province, Luding County lies between the eastern slope of Mount Gongga and the western foot of Mount Erlang, with the Dadu River running through from north to south. In ancient times, Luding was the only access from Sichuan Province to the areas inhabited by Zang people. As a major crossing point on the Dadu River, there were only bamboo ropes connecting the two river banks. Horsemen and merchants used to slide down the ropes to cross the river. In winter when the water level was low, they would ford the river in leather boats. In the 44th year of the reign of Emperor Kangxi of the Qing Dynasty (1705), the Emperor ordered a chain bridge be

泸定桥的建成也使泸定县很快成为商贸繁荣的市镇。在桥的东岸，曾是边茶交换麝香、皮毛、药材的市场，它吸引了许多藏族商贩从康定来到这里交易。

- **大渡河上的泸定桥** (图片提供：FOTOE)

泸定桥结构特殊，造型别致。桥身由13根碗口粗的铁链组成，其中底链9根，扶手4根。每根铁链由862—977节铁环组成，均由熟铁锻造。桥身净长101.67米，宽2.9米，犹如13条巨蟒横跨在波涛汹涌的河面上，令人惊叹不已。

Luding Bridge over the Dadu River
Luding Bridge has a special structure and an elegant shape. It is made of 13 iron chains, with 9 supporting the deck and the other four serving as handrails. Each chain has a diameter—the size of a rice bowl and consists of 862 to 977 interlocked wrought-iron links. The bridge is 101.67 meters long and 2.9 meters wide and looks very impressive, like 13 reclining giant pythons across the surging river.

built for military and trade purposes. He named the bridge "Luding Bridge" and wrote the name in his own hand.

After the completion of the Luding Bridge, it became an important passage from Sichuan Province to the Qinghai-Xizang Plateau, a traffic artery on the Ancient Tea-horse Road. Caravans and porters were spared from risking their lives to take a wooden boat through the deep and swift flowing Dadu River. This bridge also enabled the county to boom into a thriving commercial center. On the east bank of the river, there used to be a market where people traded tea for musk, furs, and medicinal herbs. Many Zang merchants from Kangding were attracted to do business here.

> 川西门户松潘

松潘县位于四川省阿坝藏族羌族自治州东北部，古名"松州"，是历史上有名的边陲重镇，被称作"川西门户"。早在北宋时期，松潘就已经成为汉族与藏族贸易的市

● 松州古城城门
The Gate of the Ancient Town of Songzhou

> Songpan: Gateway to Western Sichuan Province

Located in the northeastern part of the Aba Zang and Qiang Autonomous Prefecture of Sichuan Province, Songpan was known in ancient times as Songzhou. It was a well-known border town of strategic importance and the gateway to western Sichuan. As early as in the Northern Song Dynasty, Songpan had already developed into a trade market where Han People and Zang people carried out barter trade with their tea and horses respectively. During the Ming Dynasty, the market at Songpan was unprecedentedly ourishing. The western route Border Tea from Sichuan Province was first shipped to Songpan County before shipped further to the areas inhabited by Zang people in Qinghai and Gansu provinces, in exchange for

松潘黄龙钙化彩池
Calcification of Color Pool in Huanglong Scenic Area, Songpan County

场，以川茶换取藏马。至明代，松潘茶马互市空前兴盛，四川边茶中的西路边茶往往先运到松潘，再由松潘运往青海、甘肃的藏族聚居区，从藏民那换取马匹等物资。除了茶叶和马匹，交换的物资还包括牛羊肉、酥油、盐巴、药材，当时的松潘城是"烟火万家，俯视即见"，到了清朝更是"人烟稠密，商贾辐辏，为西陲一大都会"，成为川、甘、青三省边境最大的贸易集散地。马帮在松潘茶马互市历史上占有非常重要的地位，当时交通不便，进出松潘的物资全靠马帮来运输。

horses and other materials. In addition to tea and horses, people exchanged all sorts of products, such as beef, mutton, butter, salt and herbs. Back then, the town was already home to ten thousand families. And in the Qing Dynasty, it grew into a densely populated and commercially active frontier settlement in western Sichuan and the largest trade and distribution center in the border areas among Sichuan, Gansu and Qinghai provinces. Historically, caravans played an important role in local tea and horse trade, for transportation conditions were dreadful, people had to rely on caravans to ship goods in and out of the region.

> "最高城镇"理塘

理塘县位于四川甘孜藏族自治州的西南部，坐落在四面环山的毛垭草原上，海拔4700米，有"世界最高城镇"之称。理塘是四川西南地区的交通要冲，也是川藏茶马古道上的重镇，从明清

> Litang: "The Highest City"

Located in the southwestern part of the Ganzi Zang Autonomous Prefecture of Sichuan Province, Litang County lies on the Maoya Grassland surrounded by mountains. At the elevation of 4,700 meters, Litang is known as the world's highest city. It was a major town on the

• **清雍正帝颁赐七世达赖喇嘛的金印**

七世达赖喇嘛（1708-1757）名叫格桑嘉措，出生于理塘，8岁即被认定为六世达赖仓央嘉措的转世灵童，正式在理塘寺出家。七世达赖喇嘛在位期间，是西藏地区政教合一制度确立的时期，也是清廷和西藏关系最为融洽的时期。

Gold Seal Granted by Emperor Yongzheng of the Qing Dynasty to the Seventh Dalai Lama

Born in Litang, the seventh Dalai Lama Kelsang Gyatso (1708-1757) devoted himself to the religious belief at the Litang Temple, at the age of eight when he was identified as the reincarnation of the sixth Dalai Lama Tsangyang Gyatso. The reign of the seventh Dalai Lama was the time when Xizang adopted the theocratic system whereby political power and religious rule merged. This was the period when Xizang enjoyed the most harmonious relationship with the Qing Goverment.

● **理塘寺** (图片提供：FOTOE)

理塘寺坐落在理塘县城北的托洛纳卡山西麓，体势巍峨，金碧辉煌，20多座佛殿、经堂，20多座活佛宫室，400多座僧舍依山层叠，呈阶梯式排列，形成一组独特、严谨、壮观的建筑群落。寺中僧侣近4000人，在藏族聚居区声誉极高，成为康巴地区藏传佛教格鲁派的圣地。

Litang Temple

Situated on the lower western hillsides of Mount Tuonuonaka north of the county seat of Litang, the Litang Temple consists of a group of magnificent architectures, including more than 20 temples, 20 Tulku memorials, 400 dormitories in a cascade arrangement on the mountain slope. The sight is spectacular. The temple accommodates nearly 4,000 monks and enjoys a high reputation among the areas inhabited by Zang people. It is regarded as the Holy Land in Zang Buddhism by members of the Gelugpa sect in Kamba area.

时期直到现在，产于四川的川茶源源不断地输入藏族聚居区，理塘是途中的必经之地。

城北的理塘寺（又叫长青春科尔寺）是三世达赖于1580年修建的。七世达赖、十世达赖、五世嘉木样呼图克图，七世、八世、九

Ancient Tea-horse Road between Sichuan and Xizang as well as a transportation hub in southwestern Sichuan. Ever since the Ming and Qing dynasties, continuous shipment of tea from Sichuan to the areas inhabited by Zang people all had to go through this town.

In the north of the town there

世帕巴拉呼图克图，三世哲布尊丹巴，一世、二世香根活佛等这些藏传佛教领袖、活佛都降生于此。最令人难忘的是六世达赖仓央嘉措曾在一首诗中提到过理塘："白羽的仙鹤啊，借给我你的翅膀，我不会飞得太远，只到理塘便折回。"后

- **理塘草原**

在理塘县城以西的群山的环抱之中，如海的草原郁郁葱葱，这就是毛垭大草原。草原地势平坦，视野广阔，鲜花繁茂，被誉为川西最美的草原。

Litang's Grassland

West of the county seat of Litang and surrounded by mountains, there is a vast grassland known as the Maoya Grassland. Open, flat and lush, this grassland is known as the most beautiful one in western Sichuan.

stands the Litang Temple (also known as Changqingchunke'er Temple), which was built in 1581 by the third Dalai Lama. The town is also the birthplace of quite a few religious leaders and Living Buddhas (Tulkus), including the seventh and the tenth Dalai Lama, the fifth Jamyang Shêpas, the seventh, eighth and ninth Pakpalha Khutuktu, the third Jebtsundamba Khutuktu, and the first and second Xianggen. The sixth Dalai Lama Tsangyang Gyatso once wrote a poem, saying that, "Dear white feathered crane, please lend me your wings. I won't fly to a faraway place, only to Litang and return." It is believed that Tsangyang Gyatso implied in this poem that his reincarnation might be found in Litang. And as a matter of fact, the seventh Dalai Lama was found there.

Litang's grassland is a well-known pasture. When summer comes, flocks of cattle and sheep roam about on the green grassland. And people are excited about the upcoming annual event

人认为，仓央嘉措在这首诗中暗示了他将在理塘转世。后来的七世达赖果然在理塘找到。

  理塘草原是有名的牧区。夏日，草原上绿草如茵，牛羊遍地，一年一度的草原赛马会就在这里举行。七月下旬，人们便陆续将各种生活用品搬到离县城不远的草原上，搭起一座座白色帐篷。八月一日，赛马会正式开始。赛马活动一般分竞走和马上技巧两类。赛马场是康巴汉子展示才华的好机会。他们一个个身着节日盛装，腰佩长刀和各种饰物，显得十分英俊潇洒、原始粗犷。赛马场上，骑手们纵马驰骋，引起欢声雷动。赛马会期间，还要表演藏戏，举办民族体育竞赛，开展民族物资交易活动。

of horse racing. In late July, people start to pack their stuff and move into white tents put up on the grassland not far from the county seat. The event starts on the first day of August and consists of horse racing and horsemanship competitions. The racetrack is the arena for Kamba men to display their talents. In their festive costumes, toting long knives and dazzling accessories around their waists, Kamba men look handsome and attractive, rugged and tough. On the racing tracks, they compete with each other riding on their stallions, wearing swords and rifles, demonstrating their best skills and bravery, earning thunder-like applause. During the event, other activities such as Zang opera performances, ethnic games and trade fairs also take place.

> 古道盐都盐井

西藏芒康县的盐井镇，紧靠澜沧江，镇子两侧都是4000多米的高山。沿江两岸三叠纪红色沙砾层有盐泉流出，其盐泉含盐量高达30.7克/升。因此，盐井以产盐而闻名藏族聚居区，拥有世界上独一无二的古老制盐术。千百年来的积淀使这里成为藏族聚居区的富庶之地，同时也是茶马古道上的重要驿站。在茶马互市的时代，盐井是茶马古道从云南进入西藏后的第一个驿站，是横断山区举足轻重的物资集散地。当年，商队和马帮从这里经过，将滇茶销往西藏，换回兽皮、藏药，盐井所产的食盐也由此销往西藏地区。

这里的男人们都赶着骡马贩

> Yanjing: Salt Town on the Ancient Road

The Town of Yanjing, Markam County lying by the Lancang River is flanked on both sides by mountains of more than 4,000 meters high. Along the river banks, salt springs with salt concentration up to 30.7 grams per liter, flow out of the red Triassic gravel. Hence, the town is known as a salt producing site employing a unique ancient production method in the areas inhabited by Zang people. Thanks to the accumulation of wealth through the years, Yanjing became a land of wealth and an important post on the Ancient Tea-horse Road. When the tea and horse trade was active, it was the first post in Xizang on the Yunnan-Xizang Route and an important distribution center in the Hengduan Mountains. During the Tea-horse Mutual Trade period, caravans and

● 澜沧江西岸的红盐井 (图片提供：FOTOE)

令人称奇的是，尽管同取一江之水，两岸的盐田却呈红、白两色。西岸的加达村盐田是红色，而东岸上下盐井村的盐田为白色，它们分别称为红盐井和白盐井，这种现象的产生是由于两岸土质的不同——西岸用红土铺盐田，而东岸用细沙或白土铺田。

Red Salt Gardens on the West Bank of the Langcang River
What is amazing is that although the brine comes from the same river, salt gardens on the banks present different colors. The ones on the west bank (Jiada Village) look red (hence the name red salt gardens) while the ones on the east bank (Yanjing Village) look white (white salt gardens). This is because the clay used to build the gardens is different—people use local red clay to build the gardens on the west bank and fine sand or white clay on the east bank.

盐卖茶，于是，并不轻松的制盐工作就成了女人的事。当地人将江边盐泉的泉口扩大，同时就地势在泉口上修建盐棚。盐棚依岸而建，高1.8—2米，方形平顶，顶盖为10厘米厚的不透水红黏土层，四周略高，如同盐池，用以晒盐。每天早晨女人们背着桶，挑着担子下到江边的

merchants stopped at Yanjing on their way to Xizang, selling tea from Yunnan Province in exchange for animal hides and Zang medicine. At the same time, locally produced salt was shipped out to Xizang.

As local men were always on the road for salt and tea business, salt production — a job that was by no means easy — became the responsibility of

卤水井取出卤水，再挑上半山腰倒在盐田里。借着日晒风吹和盐田渗漏，卤水得以蒸发、结晶，10多天后，一层层结晶盐出现。用木刮刀轻轻刮拢这层晶体，再装到竹背篓里沥干水分即可。

women. Local people enlarged the mouth of the riverside salt springs and built salt gardens against the cliffs. These simple, flat-top buildings were 1.8 to 2 meters high, covered with a 10-centimeter thick impermeable red clay layer with a slightly higher clay fence around. Every morning, women carried buckets to fetch brine and poured it in these salt gardens. By evaporation, salt crystallized in about ten days. And with the help of a wooden scraper, the salt was collected into bamboo baskets to get dried completely before getting ready for use or sale.

• **盐井镇的天主堂**

盐井天主堂是西藏唯一的天主教堂，于1855年由法国传教士创建，教堂建筑风格兼具汉、藏和西洋风格。教堂中珍藏的藏文版《圣经》及《圣母玛利亚传记》为西藏仅有的保存完整的藏文版天主教经书。

Catholic Chapel at Yanjing Town

As the only Catholic chapel in Xizang, the Catholic chapel built in 1855 by French missionaries at Yanjing has incorporated Western, Han and Zang architectural styles. The Zang language version of the Christian Bible and Biography of Virgin Mary are the only well-preserved complete Zang language-version Catholic scriptures in Xizang.

澜沧江上的溜索

在茶马古道上，有众多的河流阻碍着商旅和马帮的行走，为了渡过那些峡谷中的湍急的河流，先民创造了一种飞跃天堑的索桥，也称"笮桥"。笮桥最早是用竹篾拧成一根粗大的绳索，系于河谷两岸，借助木制溜筒，依赖重力把人畜滑向对岸，俗称"溜索"。笮桥作为茶马古道上的一项奇观，曾使古今文人赞叹不已。澜沧江由西藏盐井进入云南境内后，江面狭窄，水流湍急，无舟船可渡，长期以来人马全靠竹篾溜索过江。过江的人将身体用绳索捆绑在形如筒瓦(溜筒)的涓桫上，从溜索一端凭借惯性往对岸滑行。"过溜"时无论人畜都心惊胆战、魂飞魄散，每年人和财物的损失不计其数。

Sliding Cables over the Lancang River

On the Ancient Tea-horse Road, many rivers crisscrossed the roads taken by business travelers and caravans. To cross such surging rivers running in deep canyons, people invented a primitive form of a cable bridge (also known as narrow bridge) to facilitate the crossing in old days. They used bamboo splints to make a thick rope and tied it on both banks. With the help of gravity, a wooden slide tube helped people and animals slide down the cable to the other side. Hence the bridge was commonly known as sliding cables. Travelling on the Ancient Tea-horse Road, men of letters, ancient and contemporary, have all been amazed at the sight of these narrow bridges.

As the Lancang River enters Yunnan Province at Yanjing Town, the water becomes narrow and fast-flowing, making it impossible to cross in boats. People had to rely on these cable bridges. They fastened themselves to the sliding tube and slid down the cable to the other side of the river. Such a ride was usually a frightening experience both for men and animals, incurring huge loss of lives and properties every year.

• 大江上的溜索
The Sliding Cable over the River

> 两河交汇之处昌都

昌都，在藏语中意为"两河交汇处"。这座历史悠久的西藏东部重镇位于澜沧江上游的谷地之中，恰好是川藏公路的中心点。自清末

- 河流交汇处的昌都城
  The Town of Qamdo at the Confluence of Two Rivers

> Qamdo: Town at the Confluence of Two Rivers

In the Zang language, Qamdo means the place where two rivers converge. As a historical town in eastern Xizang, Qamdo lies in the valley of the upper reach of the Lancang River. It happens to be at the middle point of the Sichuan-Xizang Highway. Since the late Qing Dynasty when the local government replaced Aboriginal Offices, Qamdo has been the political, economic, cultural and transportation center in eastern Xizang. Hence Qamdo has been reputed as Gateway to Eastern Xizang. Starting from Sichuan Province and Yunnan Province

- **昌都强巴林寺**

强巴林寺建于明正统九年（1444年），由藏传佛教格鲁派创立者宗喀巴大师的弟子喜绕松布主持修建。从清康熙年间起，该寺主要活佛受历代皇帝的册封。该寺主要建筑保存完好，经堂内塑有数以百计的各类佛像和高僧塑像，上千平方米的壁画以及众多的唐卡画，堪称康藏地区的艺术宝库。

The Qiangbalin Temple, Qamdo

The Qiangbalin Temple was built in the 9th year of the Zhengtong Period of the Ming Dynasty (1444) coordinated by Xirao Songbu, a disciple of the Great Master Tsongkhapa, founder of the Gelug Sect of Zang Buddhism. From the reign of Emperor Kangxi of the Qing Dynasty, emperors ordained high-ranking Living Buddhas in this temple. The main buildings have been well preserved. There are hundreds of images and statues of Buddha and high-ranking monks in the halls, thousands of square meters of mural paintings and many thangka paintings. Indeed the temple deserves to be the art treasure house of the Kamba region.

改土归流置昌都府以来，昌都市便一直是藏东地区的政治、经济、文化和交通中心，享有"藏东门户"的盛誉。茶马古道两条路线分别自云南和四川出发，穿越横断山脉以及金沙江、澜沧江、怒江、雅砻江向西延伸，在昌都交汇。

昌都市平均海拔在3500米以上，不少山峰都耸立于雪线之上。这里有藏传佛教格鲁派在康区的第一寺——强巴林寺，噶玛噶举派的祖寺噶玛寺。除藏传佛教的寺院之外，还有天主教和伊斯兰教教堂，更有三江

respectively, the two routes of the Ancient Tea-horse Road run westwards through the Hengduan Mountains and across the Jinsha, Lancang, Nujiang and Yalong rivers, and converged in Qamdo.

With an average elevation of 3,500 meters, Qamdo has many peaks above the snowline. It accommodates chapel and mosque as well as temples of Zang Buddhism, e.g. the Qiangbalin Temple, the first temple of the Gelug Sect in the Kamba area, Karma Temple, the ancestral temple of the Karma Kagyu Sect. There is also amazing landscape

并流的奇绝风景和神秘壮美的茶马古道。神奇而壮丽的自然景观和积淀着浓厚历史文化的人文景观一起构成了昌都丰富的旅游资源。

shaped by the Three Parallel Rivers and the mysterious trails of the Ancient Tea-horse Road. The spectacular natural landscape and the historical and cultural sites jointly constitute the rich tourist resources of Qamdo.

- **昌都邦达草原**

  邦达草原位于昌都市三江流域的高山深谷之中,是一块地势宽缓、水草丰美的高山草原,广阔的滩地上绿草如茵,牛羊成群。这里也曾经是茶马古道的必经之地。

  Bangda Grassland, Qamdo City

  Stretching out in a deep valley of the three-river basin at Qamdo, Bangda Grassland is open, flat and lush alpine grassland where flocks of cattle and sheep roam around. It was also on the Ancient Tea-horse Road in ancient times.

改土归流

　　元明时期，中国西南的少数民族地区普遍实行土司制度，土司拥有自己的武装，对边疆的稳定也十分不利。从明代末期开始，朝廷逐渐在少数民族地区废除世袭土司，改用政府任命的"流官"统治，简称"改土归流"。改土归流在清雍正年间云贵总督鄂尔泰任职期间得以大规模推行，在原土司领地分别设置府、州、厅、县，委派有任期、非世袭的流官进行直接统治，实行和内地一样的各项制度。这一政策对加强官员廉政建设，发展地方经济，加强中央政府的统治起了一定的作用。

Bureaucratization of Native Officers

Back in the Yuan and Ming dynasties, the Aboriginal Office System was adopted in some areas inhabited by ethnic groups in southwest China. As the armed forces owned by Aboriginal Offices posed a major threat to the stability in the border areas, the central government of the late Ming Dynasty phased out the power of Aboriginal Offices and replaced them with randomly-appointed governors. This has been referred to as the Bureaucratization of Native Officers, implemented on a large scale during the tenure of Ortai, the Yunnan-Guizhou Governor who was appointed by Qing Emperor Yongzheng. The tiered administrative structure of prefecture, sub-prefecture, and county was introduced, non-hereditary governors appointed on a limited term, and local people governed in the same way as residents in the interior. To some extent, this policy played a positive role in pushing forward the government's anti-corruption campaign, promoting local economic growth and strengthening the rule of the central government.

- 鄂尔泰画像
  A Portrait of Ortai(1677-1745)

> 日光之城拉萨

拉萨市位于西藏东南部，作为西藏自治区的首府，拉萨长期以来就是西藏政治、经济、文化、宗教的中心，是一座具有1300多年历史的古城。"拉萨"在藏语中为"圣

> Lhasa: The Sunshine City

Situated in the southeast of Xizang and with a history of 1,300 years, Lhasa, capital of the Xizang Autonomous Region, has long been the political, economic, cultural and religious center of Xizang. In the Zang language, Lhasa

- 布达拉宫

布达拉宫屹立在拉萨市区西北的红山上，是一个规模宏大的宫堡式建筑群，初建于公元7世纪，是吐蕃首领松赞干布为迎娶文成公主而兴建的。17世纪重建后，布达拉宫成为历代达赖喇嘛的冬宫居所，也是西藏政教合一的统治中心。整座宫殿具有鲜明的藏式风格，依山而建，气势雄伟。

Potala Palace

Standing on the Red Mountain to the northwest of Lhasa city proper, the Potala Palace consists of a group of impressive castle buildings. It was first built in the early 7th century by the Tubo King Songtsän Gampo for his Queen—Princess Wencheng of the Tang Dynasty. After the reconstruction in the 17th century, the Palace was used as the winter residence for the Dalai Lamas and became therefore the theocratic center in Xizang. Built on hillsides in a distinctive Zang architectural style, the whole Palace looks splendid and magnificent.

• 大昭寺

大昭寺位于拉萨市老城区的中心，距今已有1300多年的历史，是西藏现存的最辉煌的吐蕃时期建筑，开创了藏式平川式的寺庙布局规式。从古至今，大昭寺都是西藏重大佛事活动的中心，在藏传佛教各派别中都拥有至高无上的地位。

Jokhang Temple

Located in the center of the old town of Lhasa and with a history of 1,300 years, the Jokhang Temple is the most splendid architecture left from the Tubo Kingdom time. It is also the first Zang temple complex built in *Pingchuan* fashion. Since ancient times, the temple has been used as the venue for important Buddhist functions. So it enjoys the supremacy position among all the sects of Zang Buddhism.

地"或"佛地"之意，长期以来就是西藏政治、经济、文化、宗教的中心。拉萨古称"惹萨"，相传公元7世纪唐朝的文成公主嫁到吐蕃时，这里还是一片荒草沙滩，后为建造大昭寺和小昭寺用山羊背土填卧塘，寺庙建好后，传教僧人和前来朝佛的人增多，形成了以大昭寺

stands for the Holy Land or Buddha's Land. In ancient times, Lhasa was known as Resa. It is said that Resa was only a desert when the Tang-dynasty Princess Wencheng married Tubo King Songtsän Gambo in the 7th century. Later, monks had goats carry earth to fill the Wotang Lake for the construction of the Jokhang and the Ramoche temples. The

为中心的旧城区雏形。同时，吐蕃首领松赞干布又扩建宫室（今布达拉宫），显赫的高原名城从此形成。"惹萨"也逐渐变成了人们心中的"圣地"。如今，在以布达拉宫和八廓街为中心的拉萨城里，各式建筑星罗棋布，颇具民族风格的房屋和街道里聚集着来自藏族聚居区各地的人们，许多人穿着本民族的传统服装，转经筒和念珠从不离

completion of the two temples attracted missionaries, monks and pilgrims to the area. Together they helped shape the old town around the Jokhang Temple. Meanwhile, the Tubo King Songtsän Gambo expanded his palace to the present day Potala Palace, making the town prominent on the plateau. Resa gradually became the Holy Land in the minds of people. Today, the city proper around Potala Palace and Barkhor Street is teemed with ethnic style buildings and people in traditional costumes, who have come from all parts of the areas inhabited by Zang people. Many hold beads and prayer wheels in their hands. The city is steeped in ethnic

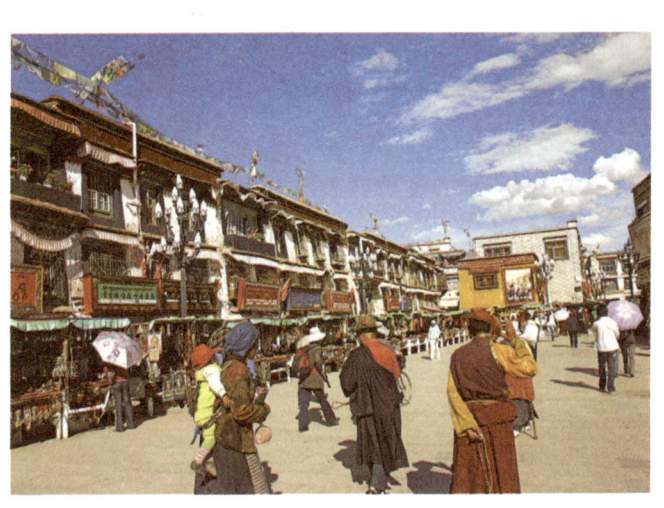

- 拉萨市内繁华的八廓街 (图片提供：FOTOE)

八廓街又名"八角街"，位于拉萨市旧城区。信奉藏传佛教的藏族民众以大昭寺为中心顺时针绕行，称为"转经"，表示对寺内释迦牟尼佛像的朝拜。八廓街原只是围绕大昭寺的转经道之一，被称为"圣路"，后逐渐成为旧城区的商业中心，较完整地保存了古城的传统面貌和居住方式。

Busy Barkhor Street, Lhasa

The Barkhor Street is in the old town of Lhasa. Usually, Zang Buddhist disciples would walk clockwise around the Jokhang Temple (praying in a circle), as a way of paying homage to the statue of Sakyamuni Buddha enshrined in the temple. As Barkhor Street was on one of the circling routes, it was referred to as the Holy Road. Later, the Street developed into the commercial center of the old town. On this street, ancient buildings are well preserved for people today to learn about how the old town looked like and how local residents lived.

手，城内处处展现出浓郁的民族风情和宗教氛围。

茶马古道上的马帮一路上历尽千辛万苦，终于走到高原圣城拉萨。在这座日光之城，大部分马帮结束了这次的旅程，恢复了元气，又开始计划下一次的行程。然而对于一部分马帮来说，行程并没有结束，他们的目的地在喜马拉雅山背后遥远的印度和尼泊尔。

customs and religions.

After a very hard journey on the Ancient Tea-horse Road, most caravans reached their destination — Lhasa where they unloaded goods and got some rest before setting out on the return journey. However, for some caravans, the Sunshine City was just another stopover post, as their destinations, India and Nepal, were still far away behind the Himalayas.

雅鲁藏布江大拐弯

　　雅鲁藏布江是世界上海拔最高的大河之一，发源于西藏西南部喜马拉雅山北麓的杰马央宗冰川，由西向东横贯西藏南部，绕过喜马拉雅山脉最东端的南迦巴瓦峰转向南流，经巴昔卡出中国国境。大江的上游和中游河段水面宽阔、水流平缓，而下游穿行于高山峡谷中，在逐渐折向东北流后，骤然急转南流，在大拐弯处形成著名的底项大峡谷。在这道举世闻名的马蹄形大拐弯中，叠套着八十余个马蹄形小拐弯，自上而下镶嵌着一个接一个的小峡谷。如此地貌奇特的峡谷，这样大的突然拐弯，在世界河流景观中实属罕见。也正是因为这个原因，雅鲁藏布江带着暖湿气团造福于林芝市，将其变成气候宜人的"西藏江南"。

The Big Bend of the Brahmaputra River

The Brahmaputra River (Yarlung Tsangpo River), one of the great rivers in the world running at the highest elevation, originates from the Chema-Yungdung glacier located on the northern hillside of the Himalayas in southwestern Xizang. It runs from west to east across southern Xizang, starts to head south after passing the easternmost Namjagbarwa peak of the Himalayas, and drains out of the Chinese border at Pasighat. The river is wide and the water flow is gentle in the upper and middle reaches. The downstream course passes deep canyons, runs further northeast before pivots southwards suddenly, carving out the famous grand canyon at the Big Bend. This hoof-shaped bend consists of more than 80 hoof-shaped small turns, crossed by an array of small valleys. It is quite an unusual river course. And such an extraordinary geography benefits the local Nyingchi area as the river brings about warm and humid air masses that contribute to the agreeable local climate and help create a "Jiangnan (areas south of the Yangtize River) in Xizang".

雅鲁藏布江大拐弯
The Big Bend of the Brahmaputra River

> 山顶庄园日喀则

　　日喀则位于西藏西南部,雅鲁藏布江与其主要支流年楚河的汇流处,藏语意为"山顶庄园",是一座古老的城市,距今已有600多年的历史。作为历史文化名城,日喀则曾是后藏地区的政治、宗教、文化中心,也是历代藏传佛教领袖班禅的驻锡之地。日喀则地处河谷地带,日照充足,农业发达,是"西藏的粮仓"之一。从拉萨沿雅鲁藏布江溯流而上,沿途有西藏三大圣湖之一的羊卓雍错,镶嵌于群山之中。而扎什伦布寺则是日喀则的象征,寺院依山而建,壮观雄伟,可与布达拉宫媲美,是历代班禅的驻锡地。该寺最宏伟的建筑是大弥勒殿,殿高30米,供奉着1914年由九

> Shigatse: A Fertile Farm

Situated in southwestern Xizang and at the confluence of the Brahmaputra River and its main tributary Nian-Chu River, the City of Shigatse, which means a Fertile Farm in Zang language, has a history of more than 600 years. This historical and cultural city was the political, religious and cultural center of the Tsang and also the residence of religious leaders Panchen Lamas of Zang Buddhism. Abundant sunshine makes the valley where Shigtse is located a great farm, known as one of the granaries of Xizang. If one travels upstream along the Brahmaputra River from Lhasa, one will find at Shigtse the Yamzho Yumco, one of the three holy lakes in Xizang, embedded in mountains. There is also the Tashilhunpo Temple, the symbol of the city. The temple is built on hillside

世班禅确吉尼玛主持铸造的弥勒坐像，总高26.2米，共用黄铜231400斤，黄金6700两，佛像两眉镶嵌大小钻石、珍珠等1400多颗。这是世界上最大的铜佛坐像。

从拉萨出发的马帮继续西行，沿着雅鲁藏布江河谷行走数个日夜后，就会来到日喀则。而一部分马帮还会继续行进，翻过喜马拉雅山的垭口，前往邻国尼泊尔。

- **日喀则扎什伦布寺措钦大殿** (图片提供：FOTOE)

  措钦大殿是扎什伦布寺内最大的建筑，位于全寺的中心地带，是个庞大的复合式建筑，大殿底层大经堂可容僧众3800人，殿中主供3米高的释迦牟尼镀金佛像。

  The Coqen Hall of Tashilhunpo Temple, Shigatse

  The Coqen Hall is the largest building in the Tashilhunpo Temple. This huge composite structure stands in the heart of the temple and can seat 3,800 monks in the main chanting hall on the ground floor. It also houses a 3-meter high, gilt statue of Sakyamuni Buddha.

and looks magnificent, comparable to the Potala Palace. The temple has been the residence of successive Panchen Lamas. The 30-meter high hall of Maitreya is the most magnificent structure and houses a giant 26.2 meter high statue of the Buddha in a sitting posture. Cast in 1914 by Thubten Choekyi Nyima, the ninth Panchen Lama, the statue was made of 115.7 tons of brass and 335 kilograms of gold, with more than 1,400 diamonds and pearls inlaid in the eyebrows. It is the largest bronze seated Buddha statue in the world.

Caravans departing from Lhasa and going westwards in the Brahmaputra valley would arrive in Shigatse in a few days. From there, some would continue their journey to Nepal after crossing the Himalayas at Yakou.

班禅与扎什伦布寺

"班禅"和"达赖"齐名,是藏传佛教格鲁派的活佛及宗教领袖。"班禅"这个称号始于1645年,蒙古固始汗尊称扎什伦布寺寺主罗桑却吉坚赞为"班禅博克多"。其中"班"是"班智达"(学者)的简称,"禅"在藏语中意为"大",二字合起来意为"大师"。1713年,清朝康熙皇帝册封班禅为"班禅额尔德尼","额尔德尼"是蒙古语"珍宝"之意。从此,"班禅"这一封号就成为班禅系统的专用名称。

扎什伦布寺是西藏日喀则市最大的寺庙,位于日喀则市城西的尼玛山东面山坡上,为四世班禅之后历代班禅的驻锡之地。明正统十二年(1447年),藏传佛教格鲁派的创始人宗喀巴大师(1357—1419)的弟子、后被追认为一世达赖喇嘛的根敦珠巴(1391—1474)在后藏贵族索南桑波等人的资助下兴建寺庙,历时12年建成,定名为"扎什伦布寺"。寺内有历世班禅灵塔,各塔大小不一,塔身都饰有珍珠和玉石。每座灵塔都燃点数量不等的大小酥油灯,终年不熄。塔内藏有历世班禅的舍利,以四世班禅的灵塔最为豪华。

- **铜镀金四世班禅喇嘛像(清)**

  四世班禅名罗桑却吉坚赞(1567-1662),明末清初藏传佛教格鲁派的首领。四世班禅是西藏历史上极有影响的人物,班禅活佛转世系统就是从他开始的,他还曾为四世和五世达赖喇嘛剃度授戒。

  A Gilt Bronze Statue of the Fourth Panchen Lama(Qing Dynasty)

  Lobsang Chökyi Gyaltsen, the fourth Panchen Lama (1567-1662) was the leader of the Gelug Sect of Zang Buddhism during the late Ming and early Qing dynasties. Historically, he was a very influential figure who developed the Living Buddha (Tulku) reincarnation system and ordained the fourth and fifth Dalai Lamas.

Panchen Lama and the Tashilhunpo Temple

Panchen Lama enjoys the same esteem as Dalai Lama, as they are titles of the Living Buddha (Tulku) and religious leaders of the Gelug Sect of Zang Buddhism. The title "Panchen" first appeared in 1645 when the Mongolian Güshi Khan respectfully referred to Lobsang Chökyi Gyaltsen, the then Master of the Tashilhunpo Temple, as "Panchen Bogd". "Pan" is the abbreviated version of "Pandita" (scholars); "Chen" means great in Zang language. "Panchen" therefore means a Great Master. In 1713, Emperor Kangxi of the Qing Dynasty titled the then Panchen Lama as "Panchen Erdene" meaning "treasure" in Mongolian. Since then, the title "Panchen" has been used exclusively.

Sitting on the eastern hillside of the Nima Mountain west of the City of Shigatse, the Tashilhunpo Temple is the biggest temple in the Shigatse and the residence of all the Panchen Lamas after the fourth Panchen. In the 12th year of the Zhengtong Period of the Ming Dynasty (1447), Gedun Drupa (1391-1474), who was posthumously bestowed the title of the first Dalai Lama and one of the followers of the Great Master Tzong Khapa (1367-1419), founder of the Gelug Sect of Zang Buddhism, started to build the temple, with the financial support of Sönam Zangpo, a member of the nobilities in Tsang. And it took twelve years to complete. The temple houses Panchen pagodas for the relics of all the Panchen Lamas, which vary in size and are decorated with pearls and jade, with butter lamps burning all year round. The pagoda for the the fourth Panchen Lama is the most extravagant one.

• 康熙皇帝颁赐五世班禅的金印（清）
Gold Seal Presented by Emperor Kangxi of the Qing Dynasty to the Fifth Panchen Lama (Qing Dynasty, 1616-1911)